RICHER RELATIONSHIPS

Myron D. Rush

This book is designed for your personal reading pleasure and profit. It is also designed for group study. A Leader's Guide with helps and hints for teachers and with visual aids (Victor Multiuse Transparency Masters) is available from your local bookstore or from the publisher.

VICTOR

BOOKS a division of SP Publications, Inc.
WHEATON. ILLINOIS 60187

Offices also in
Whitby, Ontario, Canada
Amersham-on-the-Hill, Bucks, England

About the Author

Myron D. Rush is the president of Management Training Systems, a consulting firm specializing in designing tailormade training and consulting services for both secular and Christian organizations. He is co-owner of Sunlight Industries, Inc., a solar energy manufacturing firm. Mr. Rush is also author of *Management: A Biblical Approach* (also Victor). He travels extensively conducting management seminars and consulting sessions that focus on biblical principles of management. He has a master's degree in social science and education from Central Missouri State University. Mr. Rush and his wife, Lorraine, and their two children, Delphine and Ron, live in Colorado Springs, Colorado, where his two organizations are headquartered.

Unless otherwise noted, Bible quotations are from the *New International Version*, © 1978 by the New York Bible Society. Other quotations are from *The Living Bible* (LB), © 1971 by Tyndale House Publishers.

Recommended Dewey Decimal Classification: 158.2
Suggested Subject Heading: INTERPERSONAL RELATIONS

Library of Congress Catalog Card Number: 82-062438
ISBN: 0-88207-399-0

VICTOR BOOKS
A division of SP Publications, Inc.
P.O. Box 1825 • Wheaton, Illinois 60187

Contents

Foreword

Because of the personal nature of some of the material presented in this book and in our relationship seminars, people sometimes ask Myron, "How does Lorraine feel about your sharing this?"

His answer is, "I have her permission to do so because she has seen God use it in many people's lives."

Myron and I work hard at having a consistently good relationship, and I must admit it is sometimes painful to share the times that were not good. I feel that God has given Myron the ability to look back and to analyze what we experienced. Who am I to stand in the way of his sharing this information, if it helps even one other person?

People can identify with the different stages Myron describes, can determine where they are in their own relationships, and see ways to improve them. We are not the first or the only ones to experience problems in a marriage relationship, but God has allowed Myron and me many opportunities to share these experiences in order to help others.

The basic principles of relationships dealt with in this book are valuable because every individual is involved in relationships of one kind or another—with peers, family, on the job, or in marriage. Some casual relationships we can perhaps afford to walk away from or neglect. Others we cannot, except at great loss to ourselves and our associates. It is crucially important to learn how to identify and deal with different relationship styles, rather than to ignore what's happening.

The objective of this book is to help you identify various relationship styles when you are in them. Also, and just as important, it sets forth the means by which to improve your relationships.

Lorraine H. Rush

Part 1
Diagnosis

1

Relationships: We All Have Problems

I was conducting a human relations seminar for a group of Christian leaders recently when an attractive young lady approached me during a coffee break. She asked with a worried smile, "Do you know me?"

I assured her I had never seen her before.

"Good," she said. "May I talk with you somewhere in private?"

She was embarrassed, and I found out why. "I hope you don't think this strange coming from a pastor's wife, but my relationship with my husband is not what it should be. And I'm afraid it's getting worse."

Fighting back tears, she continued. "He is a marvelous man, and I love him very much. But he is so busy we don't have any time to ourselves. When he is home, it seems most of our conversations end in arguments.

"I hate to admit it," she said, "but I find myself resenting my husband, his work, and the people he works with. This must shock you coming from a pastor's wife."

Shocked? Should any of us be shocked? I don't think we should. But we should be disturbed that this young woman—and other Christians like her—think that we would be shocked.

The plain truth is that this woman is not unusual. She shares a problem that every human being has. We *all* have problems in our relationships.

Unfortunately, Christians tend to believe they shouldn't have relationship problems, so they suppress them. They hold them inside, deny them, try to avoid them; but problems don't get solved that way.

We should not believe that relationship problems are a sign of immaturity in our Christian walk. None of us should feel particularly embarrassed or think that a godly person could not have problems in his relationships with others.

Having a problem does not indicate spiritual immaturity. Suppression of, and failure to deal with, relationship problems indicates spiritual immaturity.

Relationship Problems Are Common, but Dangerous Too

As people multiply on the face of the earth so do problems in human relationships. Every culture, society, group, organization, and individual laments the plague of relationship problems. From antiquity, friendships have been destroyed, marriages broken, families ruined, business partnerships dissolved, and a multitude of wars fought because people don't get along with each other.

I believe we have little to fear from ecological and environmental imbalances wiping us out as a race. Humanity will not perish for lack of natural resources, because of changes in global weather patterns, or through some doomsday famine or disease.

Our greatest danger is from ourselves. Apart from God's intervention, man threatens to extinguish himself from the face of the earth. We seem unable to live in harmony and to relate to each other as individuals and nations. Because we don't recognize our own imperfections, don't grasp that relationships depend on forgiveness, reconciliation, and serving each other's needs, we endanger our own existence.

God is concerned about our alienation from one another.

"There are six things the Lord hates, seven that are destestable to Him: haughty eyes, a lying tongue, hands that shed innocent blood, a heart that devises wicked schemes, feet that are quick to rush into evil, a false witness who pours out lies and a man who stirs up dissension among brothers" (Prov. 6:16-19).

God hates all these things because they undermine and destroy relationships. God intended for us to have good relationships, and He hates the actions that damage relationships. He knows we can destroy ourselves and others through degenerating relationships.

This book is written to help show why relationships develop, how they form, what causes them to degenerate, and how a bad relationship can be changed into a good one. It offers practical tools for determining the status of our relationships and a step-by-step biblical process for developing and maintaining positive relationships.

The Problem Isn't Going Away

A computer research scientist recently told me, "Our work is so frustrating. By the time we are ready to market a new computer, it's obsolete. More advanced models are already on the drawing board. There appears to be no end to technological advancement." •

Assuredly, we're living in an advanced society technologically. Over 95 percent of all the scientists who ever lived are a part of today's society. However, even with our tremendous progress in the fields of science and technology, we've made little progress in getting along with each other in man's 6,000 years of recorded history.

Human beings simply don't relate easily. Most of us have problems getting along with our best friends. With our supposed maturity as civilized people, you'd think we'd have learned something. The evidence indicates we have not.

The number of divorces steadily increases, as does the crime rate. Labor and management experience extreme difficulties with each other. And the eruption of wars in every corner of the globe attests to the poor relationships between nations. We sometimes solve individual problems that strain relationships, but other problems always seem to arise. For example, money is typically considered one of the main problem areas in marriages. But look at the statistics.

According to the 1980 edition of the *Statistical Abstract of the United States,* published by the U.S. Department of Commerce, Bureau of the Census, divorce figures were getting worse while economic conditions were getting better.

In 1979, for every 1,000 people in the United States, 10.7 marriages took place and there were 5.3 divorces. That's about 1 divorce for every 2 marriages. In the publication's 1965 figures, only 2.5 divorces took place for every 1,000 people. The divorce rate more than doubled in a 14-year period. Yet people were much less prosperous in 1965 than in 1979, even taking into account the inflation.

The same publication states that 5,521 crimes were committed for every 100,000 people in the country during 1979. In 1967, only 2,990 crimes were committed for the same number of people. That's an 84.6 percent increase.

How about employment? Employment consultants generally agree that approximately 85 percent of all employee turnover in organizations is due to personality conflicts and relationship problems, not money disputes, layoffs, or any of the other typical employee-related issues.

All of these statistics remind us that we continually face problems in relationships. They suggest a further startling realization: those problems are rapidly increasing instead of decreasing.

No One Is Exempt from Relationship Problems

Thousands of years ago, the writers of the Old Testament recorded man's initial relationship to God (Gen. 1—3). This was in many ways the brightest point in man's history. He had a perfect relationship with a perfect Lord.

But man destroyed this perfect relationship by insisting on having his own way. Very soon afterward, Adam's relationship with his wife, Eve, began deteriorating.

When God confronted Adam and asked if he had eaten of the forbidden fruit, did Adam begin trying to save his relationship with God? No, he quickly placed the blame on Eve and even on God. "The woman You put here with me—she gave me some fruit from the tree, and I ate it" (Gen. 3:12).

This blame approach is a dramatic example of what's been wrong in human relationships ever since. The human race's ability to relate in harmony quickly deteriorated even further. The two sons of the once-perfect couple got into a squabble, and Cain killed Abel.

Since that time, human history has been a record of one human relationship disaster after another. Practically any problem in history can be traced to some faulty relationship.

My job as a management and human relations consultant provides the opportunity to observe and work with government and educational institutions, local churches, international Christian organizations, and private businesses. Without exception, the organizations and groups all experience severe human relationship problems.

No one is immune from such problems, not even pastors and their wives. However, the mature person faces such problems when they arise, and is committed to find a solution. The immature person, on the other hand, frequently tries to ignore the problems and avoids dealing with issues involved in the relationship.

Such avoidance of our relationship problems is not scriptural. Jesus said, "If you are offering your gift at the altar and there remember that your brother has something against you, leave your gift there in front of the altar. First go and be reconciled to your brother; then come and offer your gift." (Matt. 5:23-24).

Jesus knows that even the dedicated and committed Christian will develop problems in his relationships. Notice that He is describing a person involved in religious activity. The person is standing before the altar offering gifts to God. Thus Jesus is suggesting that no matter how "spiritually mature," you can always experience problems in relationships. He says that as we become aware of these problems we should deal with them immediately.

The Cause of Relationship Problems

Problems in relationships occur as a result of individuals being so committed to their own views, opinions, ideas, and feelings that they abuse or neglect those of others.

A popular cigarette commercial—"I'd rather fight than switch"—captures the classic selfishness of humans. The statement implies, "I am committed to my viewpoint, and I won't even consider changing my mind."

All of us have that tendency. We'd rather fight than switch. Who wants to change? We tend to favor and promote our own opinions and feelings over the opinions and feelings of others. This applies to small personal issues such as the proper way to hold a fork and to large ones such as who should rule a country.

One Saturday morning, Lorraine and I had a disagreement concerning the best way to remove frozen orange juice from a can. Orange juice, you know, is a serious matter.

Well, I used a case knife to scrape the juice from the side of the can. Lorraine preferred that I use a flat, thin-bladed metalspatula. She believed her method was better and tried to convince me to change my ways.

"You do it your way, and I'll do it my way," I told her.

"Oh, Myron! Don't be so stubborn," she said.

A brief argument followed, slowly building up a heated atmosphere, and we went on without resolving the situation. Our little spat ended up ruining the whole day.

We were committed to our own opinions. When those opinions were challenged, we became defensive and protective of our own viewpoints. I believe that it is good to be committed to your own viewpoint. But when we become defensive and protective, we have a problem. When we nurture such an attitude, we begin to attack and blatantly reject the views of others.

Paul wrote to the people in Philippi, "Do nothing out of selfish ambition or vain conceit, but in humility consider others better than yourselves. Each of you should look not only to your own interests, but also to the interests of others" (Phil. 2:3-4). Paul warned the Philippians about their selfish motives.

Webster's dictionary defines selfishness as "the exclusive consideration by a person of his own interests." Paul challenged the Philippians to avoid such an overemphasis on themselves.

I won't be able to say this enough in this book: *Failure to give consideration to the interests of others is the major cause of problems in all forms of personal relationships.* That includes relationships on the job, in the home, and among friends. All problems in relationships can eventually be traced to the problem of selfishness.

If you want to build strong relationships, avoid overemphasizing yourself. Be willing to accept other's feelings, opinions, and ideas.

It's not easy, I know. We'll discuss the typical cycle from good relationships to bad in this book, and explore how to keep coming back to good ones.

The Dynamics of Interpersonal Relationships

Relationships evolve around personal needs. People need each other. No one is really self-sufficient. Everybody has needs that can be met only through relationships with others.

Abraham H. Maslow, a famous Brandeis University psychologist, formulated a concept of human needs pyramided into a hierarchy. Maslow concluded that man's needs fall into five distinct categories: basic physiological needs, then, safety, love (by which he means attention or social relations), esteem (including self-respect), and finally, self-actualization (or fulfillment).

Maslow, however, limited his hierarchy of basic human needs to the physical and emotional. He failed to recognize as figure 1 illustrates, *a human's spiritual needs underlie and*

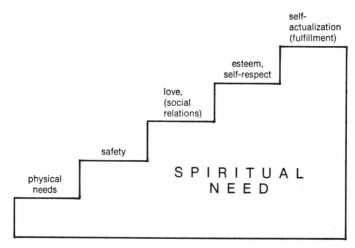

Figure 1. Man's spiritual need underlies and bridges across all his other needs.

bridge across all his other needs. As Jesus told Satan, "Man does not live on bread alone, but on every word that comes from the mouth of God" (Matt. 4:4).

In today's complex and specialized society, all of a human's needs, as formulated by Maslow, require us to form relationships with others in order to have our needs met.

For example, in order to meet our physiological needs—for food, shelter, clothing, and medical care—we seek relationships with employers who can pay us for the work we do. That's how we accumulate money to provide for our survival. The same is true of other human needs. Often, they can be met only as we form positive relationships with others.

When God created Adam and placed him in an earthly paradise, with all the food, clean air, and beauty he could desire, Adam's physical needs were met. Not only did Adam live in a perfect environment, but initially, he maintained a perfect relationship with God. All his spiritual needs were met.

Still, Adam was alone. No one shared his life and perfect environment. He was limited for personal companionship to the animals and beasts of the field. Imagine his frustration in trying to carry on a conversation with an ox, horse, bird, fish, or rabbit. That may sound romantic, but human personality traits (such as a sense of humor) need to be shared with other humans.

Adam soon realized his need for something more, soon discovered that his relationships with the animals was not exactly what could be called a fulfilling partnership. He had needs that were not being met. He needed someone of his own kind with whom he could communicate and share God's wonderful creation. God understood and said, "It is not good for the man to be alone" (Gen. 2:18). He then created Eve to be a mate, friend, and life partner for Adam.

Genesis tells us that even in a perfect physical setting and spiritual environment, a person is not fulfilled. We need relationships with other people. In God's infinite wisdom, He designed us to be physically and emotionally dependent on others. It's an interesting arrangement and a wonderful plan. The stronger our relationships with others, the more our personal needs are met. When we pull back, weakening our relationships, our needs remain unmet. This is the fundamental principle of human relationships.

Met needs build relationships. In order for relationships to be mutually rewarding, the needs of all the individuals involved must be met. As long as everyone's needs are met, the relationship grows stronger. Our goal in any relationship must be to meet the needs within the relationship.

How do we do that? How can we possibly meet all the needs within a relationship continually, thereby keeping it strong? The most important step is identifying needs as they arise. We don't maintain relationships by meeting yesterday's needs or those that existed when we began our relationship. We must meet the needs that exist right now.

The goal of any relationship, then, must be to meet existing needs.

Sometimes others don't properly identify our needs because we don't communicate them. That's the next step in meeting the needs of a relationship. We must communicate. Little is gained from identifying a need, if you're not willing to make the need known. Husbands and wives, parents and children, supervisors and employees—relationships in any sphere begin to deteriorate when needs are not communicated.

A good example is Jerry and Martha. They came to our home one Sunday evening after church for cake and coffee. As we were conversing, Jerry said, "We talked with our next-door neighbors yesterday and we may visit their church next Sunday."

This came as quite a shock to Lorraine and me, because the tone in Jerry's voice expressed "breaking some bad news." Jerry and Martha attended our church regularly.

Martha saw our surprised looks, and said, "Well, it isn't that we don't like our church. It's just that Jerry is the type of person who needs to be involved, and no one has asked him to help with any activity in the church."

"You've volunteered, and no one's interested?" I asked, quite surprised. We can always use help at our church.

"Well, not exactly," Jerry admitted. "I just assume that I'm not needed because nobody's shown any interest in my helping out."

We were all silent for a moment, as folks are when the subject matter gets a bit sticky. It was all I could do to keep from saying, "Why in the world don't you just ask if you can help?" Lorraine beat me to it.

A few weeks later after Sunday School, Martha poked Lorraine in the ribs and said, "It worked."

"What worked?" Lorraine asked.

"Jerry volunteered to teach a Sunday School class, and next week he starts assisting the teacher for the junior high boys."She smiled and said, "Just think. We were ready to start looking for another church, thinking we weren't needed or appreciated."

Something similar happened with my neighbor Charlie. "Say, who hauls your trash?" he asked one day.

When I told him, he began lamenting about the company he uses. "You know, I'm just about fed up. Lately, they don't clean up around the cans. Today, they forgot to take one of the cans altogether. I'm going to drop them and try your company. They seem to do a good job."

Nothing against the people I employ for trash collecting, but I asked Charlie if he had called and discussed the problem with his trash collectors.

"No. I just complain to my next-door neighbors," he said. We laughed about it, and another of those long pauses in conversation took place. I just smiled, and he said the words we were both thinking.

"Maybe I ought to talk to them," he said.

A few weeks later, Charlie and I were out mowing our backyards at the same time, and he came over to the fence. "You'll never believe what happened when I called my trash company," he said. "Within 15 minutes they sent a truck and a special crew to pick up the bag they left behind. A couple of days later, I even received a letter apologizing. That's the first time that ever happened to me."

He chuckled and said, "You know, I guess I've been complaining to the wrong people. I'll keep using them—now that we understand one another."

In both Jerry's and Charlie's cases, their relationships were deteriorating because they failed to make their needs known. Jerry assumed other people knew his need, and Charlie was telling his needs to someone outside the relationship. They only had to communicate their needs in order to get them met.

Of course, this will not always be the case. Unless everyone involved in the relationship is committed to meeting the needs of the others in the relationship, needs will remain unmet. Communication doesn't meet needs. It just brings them to the attention of the one who needs to meet them.

Our next principle is, *Unmet needs erode and destroy relationships.* Earlier, we said the goal of a relationship is to meet existing needs. We added that relationships will continue to grow and be strengthened as long as the existing needs are met. Unfortunately, when needs are not met, those unmet

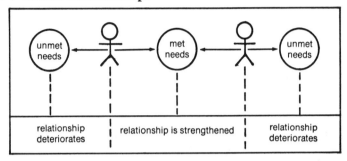

Figure 2. Unmet needs deteriorate relationships while met needs strengthen them.

needs tend to erode and destroy a relationship.

As figure 2 illustrates, two forces are working in all relationships. They are *met needs* and *unmet needs.* The diagram shows that met needs tend to draw people together and strengthen a relationship. Unmet needs tend to pull people apart and weaken their relationship. The more unmet needs in a relationship, the more distant people become. Communication tends to break down with continued unmet needs, and then more unmet needs are added to the list. The relationship becomes weaker and weaker, until eventually it can deteriorate to a point where no needs are met.

Chuck Gilmore, a friend of mine, was personnel director for an oil company. He had held that job for three years when his firm asked me to design and conduct a management and human relations course for their middle management team. During the course, we met four days a month for four months, and I slowly began to see a deep problem between Chuck and his boss.

When I told Chuck what I thought I saw, he replied, "You've seen nothing. This has been going on for six months. It has become harder and harder for us to get along with each other. I avoid him whenever I can now."

That evening, over dinner, Chuck and I talked about his needs in the relationship—needs his boss had to meet. I wanted to know what they were, and Chuck spilled them out like you'd read a shopping list.

There was lack of communication from his boss concerning the number of employees the firm planned to hire; lack of response from his boss over numerous cost-saving suggestions; failure of his boss to respond to requests for an additional employee in the Personnel Department for an increased work load; and his boss' failure to include Chuck in certain planning meetings for the future direction of the personnel department.

They weren't your petty coffee-cup and nagging-tie problems. These were real relationship issues.

"If things don't improve, I'm going to look for another job," Chuck said.

The next day, I had lunch with Chuck's boss, and asked him to describe his relationship with Chuck. The response was cold, matter of fact, and grating.

"He's one of the poorest managers I have," he said.

When I asked for his "shopping list" of complaints, I noted a similar critical tone in his response. He said Chuck needed to take more initiative in problem solving; Chuck should show more interest in and loyalty to the firm's goals; Chuck needed to accept instructions without always challenging the validity of the requests.

I let him know I'd talked with Chuck. "Are you aware that Chuck feels he needs another person in his department to assist with the increasing work load?" I asked.

'Another person?" he bellowed. "He needs another person like I need Chuck Gilmore as a manager!"

Over the next several weeks, I had the opportunity to speak at length with both Chuck and his boss, separately and together, regarding their relationship. It was a disaster. Neitherone was willing to recognize the validity of the other's needs. The result? Their needs remained unmet, and their relationship continued to deteriorate.

Two weeks after the training program was finished, Chuck called me and said he'd resigned and was taking another job.

Chuck and his boss fell into a trap many of us find ourselves in. We encounter unmet needs in our relationships.

Focusing on those unmet needs, we fail to recognize the possible needs of the other person. Eventually, one party views the relationship as hopeless and ends it. The pattern is repeated countless times in people's jobs, marriages, and friendships. Even with passing acquaintances, we may see our relationships as hopeless. Unmet needs tend to cause us to focus more on ourselves, and less on others. We become selfish, exclusively concerned with our own needs and interests. Often, our selfishness takes the form of self-pity and self-justification. We begin feeling sorry for ourselves, and justify our reactions and retaliation.

The Apostle Paul wrote, "Let us therefore make every effort to do what leads to peace and to mutual edification" (Rom. 14:19). Six verses later, he writes, "Each of us should please his neighbor for his good, to build him up" (15:2). Paul was encouraging us to focus not on ourselves, but on meeting the needs of the other person or people to whom we relate. If all the parties in relationships followed his advice, all needs in relationships would be met.

In the next chapter, we explain how meeting all of a person's needs is practically impossible. But we'll show how we must strive toward that goal anyway. The message of the Bible is clear on this, and we need to be aware of the flux of needs in relationships to see Paul's wisdom.

Four of the Ten Commandments deal with our relationship with God. The remaining six deal with our relationships with each other. All the commandments, then, deal with relationships. This should tell us something of their importance in God's sight. It also suggests our need for training in how to relate effectively both to God and to our fellow human beings.

2

The
Relationship Cycle

In my freshman year of junior college at the end of the spring semester, I had to stay on campus for a few days to wait for my father to pick me up. I was alone, and an empty school campus has to be the most boring place in the world! For three days I just wandered around.

Whiling away one lonely afternoon by walking along a deserted sidewalk, I noticed someone coming from a distance. I don't normally watch for people walking in my direction, but the silence and loneliness was awful and I got excited just seeing another person. I was even more excited when I could see that this person was a girl.

I started walking faster, eager to grasp the opportunity to talk with somebody. As I got closer, I recognized her. She was a girl I had tried to date a number of times during the year. She had always turned me down.

My heart sank for a moment, then jumped, because I knew she must also be feeling lonely on this deserted campus. We had complementary needs. I went right up to her, and, after a brief exchange of smiles and hellos, I asked her straight off what she was doing that night.

As I had guessed, she answered, "Why, nothing!"

"Would you like to get something to eat," I asked, "and

maybe catch a movie afterward?"

"Yes, I'd love to," she said. She was as eager to do something with another human being as I was.

I asked her where she wanted to eat, and she chose a Chinese restaurant. I also let her select the movie we would see. In fact, I spent the entire evening focusing on her needs, something I didn't do typically as a self-centered teenager.

A mutual trust developed between us that night because we were meeting each other's needs. In a mutual trust relationship, cooperation becomes the rule, because the other person's needs come first. We don't worry about our needs, because the partner in the relationship is meeting our needs. With people acting like that on both sides of the relationship, everyone's needs are met.

That was a terrific evening for me, and for Lorraine. We were mutually happy with each other. Our relationship grew. We dated each other often after that, continually striving to meet each other's needs.

However no relationship stays at this wonderful mutual cooperation level. Sooner or later we begin to lose sight of meeting each other's needs and begin to look at ourselves. Our needs are unmet somehow, and we begin to focus on a remedy for that situation.

That happened with Lorraine and me, and our quickly developed relationship slowly deteriorated over the years. I'll finish the story in a moment.

When we lose sight of the partners in our relationships, we take the first step away from cooperation and allow a retaliatory attitude to develop toward the person not meeting our needs.

One person cannot maintain cooperation and mutal trust for an entire relationship. Both must work at it A humble, forgiving, kind, gracious, loving, and long-suffering person will probably be misused, for when the moment comes that his partner in the relationship has an unmet need, the long-suffering one will probably be dominated.

Firm commitment to each other is essential in a good relationship. No matter what kind of relationship it is— workmate, friend, spouse, fellow church member—we must be concerned first about others to be a cooperative partner. We are naturally self-seeking, self-centered beings, so to be harmonious in our relationships we must choose to be other-seeking and other-centered.

We can't expect the ordinary course of events to keep us cooperative, nor can we "keep everything just like it is now." Relationships are constantly changing, evolving, and shifting. A healthy relationship today can begin degenerating tomorrow.

We will spend considerable time in later chapters showing how to restore relationships to steady ground. Sure change is inevitable; we must take deliberate steps to move relationships back to cooperation continually.

But now, what happens when relationships deteriorate? What is it that transfers us from living, blossoming cooperation to dead, cold, and silent isolation?

I believe a similar pattern or cycle tends to occur in all relationships. Like the four seasons, our relationships move through a series of ever-dissolving stances, though in this case the decline can be stopped. We can return to spring at any time. We don't have to go through the cold winter of isolation.

Changes in relationships come because needs in relationships also change. As one need is met by our partner, a new one takes its place.

Each new need brings with it the potential of going unmet. It also has the potential of strengthening a relationship by being one more need that is met. Each new need requires new and different ways of satisfaction. Therefore, the action required by a partner to meet one need of the other partner won't necessarily meet the next one.

It's inevitable that sometimes we'll have unmet needs. How should we respond then?

According to Scripture, we should go on meeting the other person's needs. We must not retaliate. Jesus tells us that in contrast to the concept of "an eye for an eye," we are to turn the other cheek (Matt. 5:38-39).

This most difficult of Scripture teachings to obey reveals our sinful nature. We are going to wrong each other, and just as bad, we are going to strike back when we are wronged. It's our sinful nature.

The questions we must ask ourselves is not whether we ever sin against our brother. We must ask, "How are we going to deal with the sin once it has been committed?" Shall we ignore it, pretend it doesn't exist, hope that it will just go away?

A friend of mine, in the national spotlight of Christian work, has a serious personal problem. He doesn't want anyone to know about it, afraid he will lose credibility. He is shoving his problem under the rug. And the pile under that rug is getting bigger and bigger and bigger.

He won't be able to hide his problem forever.

I know, because a similiar thing happened in my own life. Lorraine and I began with a beautiful courtship, with harmony and a meeting of each other's needs. But it didn't stay that way. It changed.

Like most people, we weren't prepared for the changes.

After our wedding, we took a honeymoon trip to Colorado. We were on the road four days, stopping to eat out, staying in motels, and getting tired of the initially exciting travel routine.

When we reached Canon City, Colorado, I saw a sign for a Mexican restaurant. I always looked for Mexican restaurant signs when it was time to eat, because I loved Mexican food.

For four days, we had eaten at Mexican restaurants, and I automatically drove into the parking lot of that Mexican restaurant.

"Myron, couldn't we eat *Chinese* food tonight?" Lorraine pleaded. For four days, she had suffered through those Mexican dinners. She had passed her limit about three days earlier, and I was just warming up.

"What's the matter with Mexican food?" I asked shocked.

"Well, we've had it every night, Myron!"

I looked around from where I was sitting, craning my neck out the back window, peering out the side windows, and then staring up at the giant Mexican restaurant sign in front of us.

"I don't see any Chinese restaurants anywhere. Besides, we're here." With that, I got out of the car and went around to escort her to another exciting evening of beans and tortillas.

My mind was on my own desires.

I wasn't interested in eating where Lorraine wanted to eat. I *had* to eat where I wanted. Lorraine and I look back now on that incident and agree that my selfishness began to deteriorate our cooperative relationship. And it happened only four days after our marriage!

Now, eating where I wanted was pretty much a subconscious act. But we both consciously became a little less interested in the other's needs as a result of that act. You see, unless we constantly focus on the needs within our relationships we may not even be aware of the changes taking place.

Failure to recognize changing needs almost guarantees that new needs will go unmet too. For example, many parents suddenly realize their relationship with a child has deteriorated, and they can't understand why. In most cases, the child's needs changed, but the parents failed to recognize the new needs.

For example, as a child grows, his need for independence grows. If parents fail to recognize this increasing need for independence (and the many other needs in a child's life), the relationship will surely begin deteriorating.

Just not meeting independence needs can cause a parent/child relationship to suffer deeply. Parents cannot expect to make the same decisions for a teenager that they made for the child ten or even five years earlier.

How about the other needs—for trust, self-esteem, attention? You can see how deterioration takes place without conscious attention to meeting needs.

The same principle applies to organizations. The things that motivate an employee while he is learning his job may not continue to motivate him once the job is learned. Supervisors must continually give attention to employees' current needs if they hope to maintain a high degree of motivation in them.

If you want to maintain a strong, healthy relationship with others, be alert to the changing needs within the relationship.

The degree of commitment to the relationship greatly influences its longevity. Therefore, another principle is: *The greater the commitment to the relationship, the better its chances are for good health, growth, and development.*

Peter once asked Jesus, "Lord, how many times shall I forgive my brother when he sins against me? Up to seven times?" (Matt. 18:21) The question underlying that was: How much commitment should be required in a relationship.

Peter suggested seven times (actually a lot to forgive when you think of actually doing it) to express his idea of what limit commitment had in a relationship.

"I tell you, not seven times, but seventy-seven times" was Jesus' reply (v. 22).

Whether the correct figure is 77 times or 490 times, Jesus is actually saying we should place no limit on how often we forgive our brother.

This passage supplies a very important principle in human relationships. We must be committed to our relationships with people, regardless of how many times they offend us. Applying that, we see that Christians should never be the ones to terminate relationships because they've been offended.

"Therefore as God's chosen people, holy and dearly loved, clothe yourselves with compassion, kindness, humility, gentleness, and patience. Bear with each other and forgive whatever grievances you may have against one another. Forgive as the Lord forgave you" (Col. 3:12-13).

Notice in this passage all the traits we should put on, emphasizing that we extend ourselves. That's commitment to others.

Commitment in relationships separates the Christian from much of the rest of the world. In obedience to Christ the Christian is committed to others in his relationships, and committed to meeting the needs of others.

By contrast, the world's philosophy is: "You only go around once, so get all you can." The world says, "Look out for your own needs, because no one else will."

If we all were committed only to our own needs, what a sad state we'd be in. What a sad state we are in!

The Four Basic Relationship Styles

Psychologists and psychiatrists categorize and label abnormal mental attitudes and the actions associated with them. Psychological terms such as paranoid, schizophrenic, and psychopathic are almost household words.

However, little has been done to analyze our everyday, "normal" relationships—to categorize various ways we relate and to identify actions associated with these ways. That's what we hope to do here.

When discussing normal relationships, we often encounter difficulty in expressing ourselves. We tend to refer to our relationships with friends, neighbors, co-workers, and loved ones as "good" or "bad."

However "good" and "bad" do little to explain what we're really trying to say. They are imprecise.

In James D. Hamilton's book, *Harmony in the Home* (Beacon Hill Press, 1977), four relationship styles are mentioned:

● Cooperation
● Retaliation
● Domination
● Isolation

I will use Hamilton's categories in our discussion of relationships.

Relationships follow a definite pattern in development and degeneration. Relationships tend to be cyclic (see figure 3). They begin with a cooperative style and remain there as long as all needs are being met in the relationship. When needs go unmet the relationship moves into a retaliation style.

Here, one or both partners try to get back at the other, to show the other person some unmet need. The relationship will continue in this style until one person "forces" the other

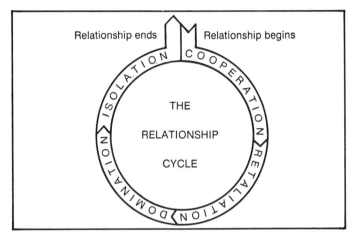

Figure 3. Relationships evolve through four stages or styles. They begin with cooperation, move to retaliation, change to domination, and finally arrive at isolation, the last style before the relationship is terminated.

to meet his need. This requires manipulation, and eventually produces a "winner."

At this point, the relationship moves into a domination style. Now the person being dominated must meet the dominator's needs in order to get his own needs met even partially. This style can't go on forever. Eventually, the dominated one begins to feel the relationship is hopeless. His needs get bypassed, met too late, or simply brushed aside.

When the dominated person concludes that the situation is hopeless, the relationship moves into an isolation style. There it remains until the relationship is terminated or until it is restored to cooperation.

We should understand that the deterioration cycle just described is typical, not inevitable. A relationship can be restored to cooperation at any point, thus checking any further deterioration for the time being. Or a relationship might remain at one of the stages of the cycle for a long period of time.

Lorraine and Myself

I spent ten years at the retaliation level with Lorraine, until I attempted to make her move to Alaska. The fish are two feet long in Alaska, and I had always dreamed of moving there. Then the opportunity came. I was offered a job in Anchorage. At that point, the strained retaliatory relationship between Lorraine and me became a "win or lose" situation.

"Isn't it great, Lorraine? Alaska!" I said, knowing she would probably react adversely. I put as much enthusiasm as I could into the announcement, to let her know I was excited.

"How far is that?" she asked me.

I told her about 4,000 miles, "up to God's country." We were living in Billings, Montana at the time.

"Oh, I wouldn't want to move that far away," she said firmly. "My parents are getting older, and it would be such a drastic change."

She didn't share my dream.

I was stuck. There was no way to get her to Alaska. I tried everything I could, cajoling her, even bribing her. Nothing worked.

I had only two alternatives, I thought. One was to acquiesce, give in, accept her unwillingness to take off to a faraway place. The other was to *make* her go, to force her to conform to my need.

I decided to take the aggressive course. I got our two children on my side, and we took a "democratic vote." But that didn't work either.

Lorraine suddenly became an object in my way. I stopped seeing her as an individual with needs I should meet. She was a block to the fulfillment of my dream. I had to control her, to squeeze her into submission.

Somebody had to lose this fight. In retaliation, we both had been fighting. Now, I needed her to lose. So I pressed as hard as I could, and I won.

"OK, Myron," she said, finally. "I don't care where we live."

Boy, she was an intelligent woman, I thought. All my pushing had been worth it. I even wondered why I had thought she was an object in my way.

Actually, her giving in was just that. She wasn't giving *me* anything. Though it looked as if I would get my need met, I little knew what was in store for us.

We moved to Alaska, and I set up shop at my new job. Things seemed great for a while. The fish really were two feet long! But progressively, my domination style threaded its way into everything I did.

At work, my employees no longer liked their initially exciting jobs. They slaved for me, doing just what I wanted. At home, my wife slaved for me, doing just what I wanted. And when Lorraine or the people at work didn't do what I wanted, I couldn't understand.

I continued my dominating style, feeling successful with it, thinking I was almost expected to use it. I suffocated my wife, bending her will toward my better judgment. In my new staff environment, I no longer had any retaliatory fights to win. They were all finished. I had the upper hand. Everyone was doing what I required.

Little did I realize that I was suffocating my wife's love for me along with her personality. Little did I realize that I was suffocating my employee's respect for me along with their creativity.

Three things mark the domination style.

1. A total lack of concern for the other person's needs.
2. A total commitment to our own needs.
3. Being the winner in the struggle for control.

A person can turn this relationship around, working to live again in the cooperative style. But we don't want to give up any ground we have fought hard to win. We have the power, so why should we surrender?

The dominator should see what is happening right away, but because everything looks so good, he doesn't. Only the one being dominated feels the pressure and says, "Something is seriously wrong here." However, getting through to the dominator takes an increasingly assertive approval as the deterioration continues. Assertiveness is impossible for the one being dominated, who is becoming weaker and weaker. Such a person now tries to satisfy the needs of the dominator just to get a few meager needs met.

For a complete return to cooperation, a relationship must achieve open and honest communication. As we said in chapter 1, good communication requires that a person tell the others in a relationship what he or she is actually feeling. But if you tell me what you really think and feel, and I reject those feelings, then you feel even worse.

We often go through life afraid to express our feelings, because of a fear of rejection. But because we are hurting, we become critical of others for not meeting our needs. We end up ignoring the other person, at which point we move into the final style—isolation.

Remember, the four-stage cycle of relationships does not have to run it full course to the end. People can interrupt the cycle at any point and restore the relationship to cooperation. In fact, restoring a relationship to cooperation is easier the earlier it is done and becomes more difficult with each progressive stage of the cycle.

As my domination of Lorraine continued, she began to feel a sense of hopelessness. Our relationship balanced on the edge of isolation.

Those were the days of the miniskirt, and I loved to see women in them. I decided my wife should wear a miniskirt, but she hated them.

I didn't care. I knew how to get my way. I took her shopping one day, impressing her with my sudden interest in her, and we went looking for new clothes for her. She was elated.

When I showed her the miniskirt rack, she said, "Oh, no, Myron. I've told you I couldn't wear one of those." She wasn't softened one bit by my "generosity." I was furious.

I picked out two I liked, went to the cashier, and paid for them—right in front of her. I was in complete control. And it went beyond her clothes. I picked her friends, her leisure activities, the parties we attended. I decided everything.

The domination style does that. But soon it does something else. It destroys our respect for each other. "I have to do everything for everyone," the dominator says. "He can't do anything I want to do," the dominated one says.

At work, I began losing respect for my employees. They lost respect for me. All the creative and innovative ideas at home and at work suffocated under my domination, and my wife and my employees didn't even want to talk with me anymore.

My staff began working behind my back. I was shocked to learn that they had called Washington, D.C. and applied political pressure to get some programs initiated that I wouldn't even consider.

The same kind of thing began happening at home. I came home one evening from work, smelled a Mexican dinner cooking, and I was ecstatic. My wife is an excellent cook of Mexican food (she's had years of experience). She was also wearing one of the miniskirts I bought her.

"I really have a good wife," I thought.

We had a delicious meal, without the children. Lorraine had someone watch them for the night. It was great! Then she disappeared for a while and came out in her sexiest nightgown. I completely forgot about the problems I had at work. I completely forgot about all the "disrespect" my wife had shown me. Things had changed!

But things hadn't changed. Lorraine was making a power play. She was setting me up to demonstrate that there was a part of our relationship I didn't control. When we reached our bedroom, she went straight to the bed and turned away from me toward the wall.

"I have a terrible headache, Myron," she said.

I exploded. I yelled at her and started stomping out of the bedroom. "You're not the only fish in the ocean," I shouted as I left. I was striking back with the meanest words I could think of.

At that point, I had been a Christian for five years. I was teaching Bible study classes at our church, and maintaining a good front. Nobody had a clue to our problem.

But the problem was becoming more complicated. Lorraine had told me in her own way that, though I made all the decisions, she still controlled a few things. We were passing out of domination into isolation.

The person being dominated usually initiates the isolation style, because the dominator is happy with things as they are. Lorraine began the move to isolation in the bedroom, but she soon began to block me out mentally as well. She got totally engrossed in television, the dishes after dinner, and her work. All communication between us stopped. She built a wall of separation, and I wasn't able to break through to her.

Then mistrust began to set in. Lorraine assumed that I really was out finding "other fish in the sea." She began communicating her mistrust of me, often without saying a word.

People at work mistrusted my actions too. I realized, like Lorraine, they had isolated themselves from me. Now all needs were going unmet—and not just the needs of those being dominated. Not only were they suffering, *I* was suffering.

The only recourse left to people in this situation—other than beginning the painful restoration process through open and honest communication—is to terminate the relationship. That's what I chose to do. One day, sitting in my office, I decided to quit. I walked into the president of the university where I was working, and handed him my resignation.

"Don't worry about renewing my contract, because I quit," I told him.

Boy, that felt good, I thought. It felt so good that the next thing I decided was to get a divorce. My job relationships were on the rocks, and I solved that problem by quitting. I might as well get my marriage over with too.

"Lorraine, I want a divorce," I told her.

I was rid of the troubled relationships. Great! Except I slowly began to realize I was also out in the cold myself.

We'll discuss in part 2 what I did about those relationships at that point. For the next four chapters, we'll examine in detail the four styles of relationships:

The Cooperation Style. The starting point for all relationships. Partners focus on meeting each other's needs.

The Retaliation Style. The first step away from cooperation. Someone in the relationship decides his or her needs might not be met, and acts to make sure they are.

The Domination Style. The emergence of a "winner." Building on the fear of not getting a need met, a person pursues aggressive action to be certain his or her needs get met first, and achieves a position of power.

The Isolation Style. A significant withdrawal, based on a feeling of hopelessness and initiated by the one being dominated. The relationship is now in serious trouble and in all probability will terminate unless steps are taken to return to cooperation.

How Long from One Style to Another?

At relationship seminars I am often asked, "How long does it take for a relationship to move from one style to another?"

The duration of a relationship style is not really predictable. Some relationships evolve through the entire four cycles in a matter of hours. Others, like mine with Lorraine, can take several years.

The length of time for a relationship style to endure depends on many factors:

● The number of people involved.
● The purpose of the relationship.
● The commitment to the relationship.
● The value of the relationship.
● The maturity level of the individuals.

The key factor in a healthy relationship is met needs, and the cause of deterioration of a relationship is unmet needs.

3

The Goal: A Cooperation Style Relationship

The Bible commands us to consider the needs of others as well as our own: "Do nothing out of selfish ambition or vain conceit, but in humility consider others better than yourselves. Each of you should look not only to your own interests, but also to the interests of others" (Phil. 2:3-4).

Jesus set forth the cooperation relationship style by saying, "In everything do to others what you would have them do to you" (Matt. 7:12).

All healthy relationships start because people have needs. When we call upon each other to meet our needs, we are saying that we can't meet them all by ourselves.

Starting relationships requires some commitment, a decision to join together in meeting each other's needs. I've never seen a man and woman walking down the marriage aisle unless they were committed to a cooperative relationship. The same is true of an employee and employer on the first day at work, or a pastor starting out with a new congregation, or a teenager on a first date.

In all these relationships, people join together to meet needs that are not being met any other way. God has given us each other, along with the free will to make these cooperative commitments. But few relationships remain in a cooperative style indefinitely.

Consider marriage partners who make strong early commitments to each other. What happens a few years later? Consider employees on the job looking for better conditions, pastors discussing their contract renewals, and teenagers a few weeks after the first date.

All of us can cite relationships that disintegrated from something beneficial and rewarding to a preview of the Battle of Armageddon.

Why Do They Start So Well?

Relationships begin in a cooperative style from the desire to meet complementary needs. As we stated in chapter 1, all people have needs that are met only through relationships with other people. Therefore, relationships must form around harmonious and complementary needs.

As figure 4 illustrates, if two of us have the same complementary need, such as friendship, we are stimulated to form a

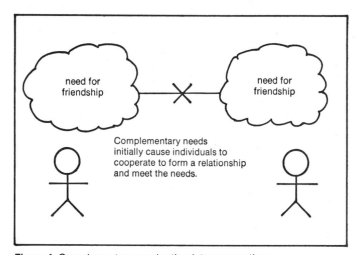

Figure 4. Complementary needs stimulate cooperation.

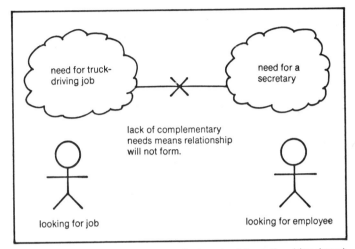

Figure 5. When complementary needs do not exist, relationships do not form.

relationship. The relationship meets our need for friendship.

However, as figure 5 shows, a relationship won't get off the ground without those complementary needs. Unless the needs in a cooperative relationship remain complementary, the relationship will stop developing in the original positive manner and begin to deteriorate.

The Apostle Paul wrote, "Each of us should please his neighbor for his good, to build him up" (Rom. 15:2). Here again, we have a biblical command to focus on a cooperation style relationship. This verse expresses the very heart of the meaning of this relationship style.

Everyone in the relationship is told to meet the needs of the others: to serve and please others, do things for others, build up, promote, and edify others. This automatically means less emphasis on self. We focus on others, not ourselves.

Initially, we voluntarily focus on meeting another's needs in a relationship, believing our own needs will be met as well. We take a risk, but it's one we are fairly comfortable about and an investment we make willingly if not eagerly.

Bill and Doris Wilberham, brand new Christians in our church, needed help and guidance in their spiritual growth. They had no idea what they could offer in return, so were hesitant about forming a relationship in which everything was "take" on their part.

Clyde and Charlotte Peterson, a spiritually mature couple in our congregation, had extensive experience in leading home Bible studies. They were new to the city and looking for friends.

You can see the compatibility or complementary nature of the Peterson's and the Wilberhams's needs. Each couple needed something that the other couple could offer.

The two couples met in a Sunday School class at church, and within a week were involved together in a Bible study. As a result, the Wilberham's need for help in spiritual growth was met, and the Peterson's friendship need was met.

Both couples were willing to venture out to form a relationship to meet their needs. Each wanted to cooperate with the other. Their needs drew them together, and the small risk involved was worth taking.

We should keep in mind that *complementary* needs do not have to be *identical* needs. The Petersons had different needs than the Wilberhams had. Needs are complementary when a single interaction meets the needs of all those involved. For the Petersons and Wilberhams, a home Bible study was the interaction that met both of their needs.

How We Look at the Start

At the time our relationships begin—and for as long as they remain in a cooperative style—we have a strong and continuing commitment to meet each other's needs. We achieve success as we:

- focus on a common goal
- place less emphasis on ourselves than on the others
- have mutual trust and respect
- solve problems jointly
- find it easy to avoid potential problems

● grow in an increasingly productive relationship
● become more strongly committed to the relationship

Cooperation style relationships require the continuation of attitudes and actions presented when a relationship starts. From the forgoing list of eight characteristics of a relationship when it starts, we can pull out six major features of a cooperation relationship:

● commitment
● common goal
● unselfishness
● mutual trust and respect
● creativity
● continued new commitments

You will find each of these positive features in your cooperative relationships at some time. Let's consider them one by one.

Commitment

First, any relationship requires a commitment to meet the other person's needs. This commitment is the key to a cooperation relationship, and the basis for forming a relationship in the first place.

Over the long haul in a relationship, people often weaken in their commitment. Social pressures today put incredible strains on people and their relationship commitments. We live in a world that questions all our commitments—to employers, friends, even to families.

For Christians, commitment is vital. When we lose sight of our commitment to each other, we immediately begin drifting apart. It happens often enough, and we need to know what to do about it.

Jesus once told His disciples about a man who was giving a big dinner for all his friends (see Luke 14:16-24). They were people to whom he was personally committed. He thought they were committed to him as well.

The man discovered he had made a wrong assumption. His "friends" gave all kinds of excuses for skipping his special celebration. One had to check out some new land he had bought, another had to take his new oxen for a spin around the pasture, and one blamed his absence on his new wife.

The friends all had "new" commitments.

Jesus described real commitment to Him when He said, "If anyone comes to Me and does not hate his father and mother, his wife and children, his brothers and sisters—yes, even his own life—he cannot be My disciple"(Luke 14:26).

Jesus didn't just give lip service to this commitment principle. He lived it, by showing us that we come first to Him. He sacrificed everything, and "hated" His own life for us.

Why don't we do that with everyone to whom we make our commitments? I believe it's because we are sinners. We tend to fudge and let our relationships slip, even taking advantage of the commitment others make to us.

When our relationships begin, we try to do whatever it takes to meet another person's need. The relationship is exciting, and the commitment comes pretty easy at first. That is good, because it gets our relationships going. But the "you first" choices lose their initial excitement after a while. The luster fades from the relationship and it turns into hard work. When we must continue to put each other first, the sinner in us surfaces.

All partners in a relationship are affected by one's sins, no matter who stops putting the other person first. For example, if I am totally committed to you, then your relationship grows as you stay committed to me. But when I drop that commitment, just for a time, I start a pendulum swinging. I begin to move away from eager commitment, and you feel the pressure. Soon I may find you have moved back a little from your commitment too.

When our partners begin putting their oxen, land, or new relationship first, we tend to hop on the pendulum. Eventually, our commitment to meet their needs begins to slip away, and the relationship is in jeopardy.

Very often, if we feel the least bit threatened by our partners, we begin to suspect our commitment because we aren't sure they are going to be committed anymore.

I was in a county agency in Colorado doing an organizational analysis on strengths and weaknesses in the agency's office. While I was talking with the man in charge of planning, his telephone rang, and he answered it. I could tell he was talking to one of the county commissioners.

The commissioner must have implied that the Planning Department was running less well than expected. When the director hung up the phone, he used some very descriptive words that translated, "If he doesn't like the way I do things, he can get somebody else."

That response is typical in relationships today. When the going gets rough, the roughed up get going.

Look at many marriages. When difficulty arises, what often happens? Our society's values encourage marriage partners to look to someone or something else to meet their needs.

A Common Goal

Complementary needs draw people together, and common goals keep people together. I consider common goals the stabilizer to long-term relationships, because unless common goals are agreed on and maintained, a relationship will eventually terminate.

In figure 6, we show the relationship of a young couple, starting out in friendship. The partners willingly commit themselves to fulfill each other's needs. But the goal changes in this relationship. One wants to go deeper, to make a commitment of marriage. The other only wants friendship.

Unless the conflict over the goal is settled, the relationship could end following a power struggle over the goal of the relationship.

We read in Psalm 133:1, "How good and pleasant it is when brothers live together in unity!" Unity in our goals is essential if we are to maintain a cooperation relationship style.

Because of the acute problem in goals and goal-setting, we will discuss this issue at length in chapter 9 when we consider what it means to work as a team. We can say here that the

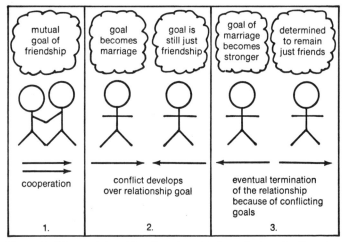

Figure 6. When relationships do not maintain mutual goals, the relationships eventually terminate.

existence of a common goal is an important factor in remaining cooperative, because goals give meaning to relationships.

Unselfishness

The cooperation style continually focuses on serving rather than being served. Of the four relationship styles discussed in this book—cooperation, retaliation, domination, and isolation—only the cooperation style focuses on serving others in the relationship.

As figure 7 shows, the other three styles focus on being served. If you are interested in developing a cooperation-based relationship, then you must begin by serving.

Serving others does not come naturally. By nature, we seek to be served. That's why we are commanded to look "not only to your own interests, but also to the interests of others" (Phil. 2:4).

The pages of history are filled with man's efforts to force others to serve his needs. Jesus drew attention to this problem, saying, "You know that the rulers of the Gentiles lord it

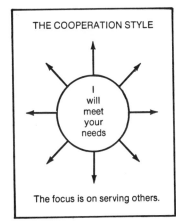
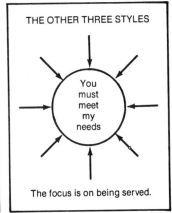

Figure 7. Relationships evolve around needs being met. In the cooperation style relationship, the focus is on meeting the needs of others (serving). In the other three styles the focus is on getting others to meet your needs (being served).

over them, and their high officials exercise authority over them" (Matt. 20:25).

In the world's system of relating, the focus is on "me first." Jesus told His disciples that they must be different. "Not so with you. Instead, whoever wants to become great among you must be your servant . . . just as the Son of man did not come to be served, but to serve, and to give His life a ransom for many" (vv. 26-28).

The person wishing to direct his relationships cooperatively must begin by committing himself to meeting the needs of others ("be your servant"), imitate Christ ("just as the Son"), and go the distance of continually meeting others' needs ("give His life").

Jesus is our ideal. Even during the crucifixion, He thought first of His oppressors: "Father, forgive them, for they do not know what they are doing" (Luke 23:34).

If we are to be like Jesus, we must not resort to "getting even." However, accepting the pain inflicted on us by our friends, spouses, and partners does not mean that we should be silent. Our silence will turn to brooding, and that does not serve the needs of others any more than retaliation does.

Some people have incredible tolerance for mistreatment. They never seem to break under pressure or complain about anything. That tolerance is good, but taking a beating without communicating your pain is both unwise and unhealthy.

Walter Flemming is a good example. He spent twenty years working his way up the ladder of success, finally arriving at the top. When I met him, he was forty-five years old and vice-president and general manager of a Kansas City manufacturing firm.

But inside the man was a mess—frustrated, unhappy, worn out.

"I'm fed up with people," he told me. "My company uses me to make a profit. My wife and family use me to pay their bills. And I just learned today that a guy I thought was a good friend has been using me to get even with his boss."

He smiled feebly, trying to brush it all off, but since he had started, he decided to just let it all out. He concluded, "Someday people are going to realize I'm like any other natural resource. They'll wake up and discover I've been all used up."

The world is probably full of people like Walter who fail to communicate their pain for fear of damaging their relationships. They behave unselfishly, but they violate the basic principle of relationships—*mutual fulfillment* of one another's needs. Since Walter's relationships were one-sided, he needed to let his partners know that.

Because he kept his unsatisfied needs inside, Walter was now actually focusing on himself. He wasn't about to explode in the typical way people end relationships. He would just disappear, and nobody would even know what happened.

Cooperation demands serving others by meeting their needs. But other people must know about our needs as well. As I have emphasized, we form relationships because we have needs we are unable to meet alone. But our needs won't get met if we are either self-centered or "selfless" in the sense of never expressing our needs. There's a paradox here: We must neither be selfish nor selfless.

If we selfishly focus on our own needs all the time, our relationships suffer. Our needs may get met for a time under these conditions, but constant turmoil and conflict will arise, and ultimately nobody's needs will be met.

On the other hand, if we "selflessly" focus on meeting other people's needs while our own needs go unmet, the very basis for the existence of the relationship comes under attack and a deterioration of the relationship is inevitable.

So a balance is required. We must focus on the needs of others, but we must also make our own needs known. When we maintain this balance, our relationships can flourish.

With most of us the tendency is probably more toward the "selfishness" error than toward the "selflessness" error. We are a bit like Frankie, a high school hockey player on the same team as my son, Ron. In order to get the recognition and respect that he needed from his friends and fellow players, Frankie wanted to be the high scorer.

In the first game of the hockey season, Frankie shot the puck at the goal every time he got it. He refused to pass to other players even when they were in the open. After all, someone else might make more goals than he and receive more recognition!

Before long, Frankie's teammates realized that he wasn't going to pass the puck, and they retaliated. They refused to pass off to him, even when Frankie was in the open. Consequently, Frankie didn't score any goals the first game, there was tension on the ice, and most of the team members were angry at him.

Frankie failed to get the recognition he needed, created enough conflict to jeopardize the game for his team, and threatened his entire relationship as a team member. That evening, the coach talked long and hard on teamwork and cooperation. Then he made it clear that uncooperative players weren't going to remain on the team long if the power struggle on the ice continued.

Frankie got the message. As a result of his selfishness in

meeting his own needs, he was about to lose a relationship he needed: being a member of the hockey team.

In the next game, Frankie was a completely different player. He worked hard at helping others to score. His cooperative behavior paid off, and other team members passed the puck to him. He didn't become high scorer for the season, but he did gain the respect and recognition he needed.

Jesus said, "Give, and it will be given to you. A good measure, pressed down, shaken together, and running over, will be poured into your lap" (Luke 6:38).

If we meet the needs of others, they will often go out of their way to meet our needs. During human relationship seminars, I frequently ask people, "What is the first thing you think of when someone does something for you?"

People usually respond, "What can I do in return?"

When Dwight and Cindy were planning to move to Phoenix, they wrote to several real estate firms in Phoenix asking for information on housing. One evening when they were at our house for dinner, I asked Dwight if any of the real estate firms had responded.

"Most of them wrote back saying that we should call them when we arrive in Phoenix," Dwight said. "Only one gave us any real help."

"But that one was amazing," Cindy said. "That firm sent us a large packet with names and addresses of all the churches; a large city map with shopping centers circled in red; the number, names, and sizes of all the schools; the major companies with positions that Dwight might want; banking firms; and even a complimentary ticket for a free dinner at one of the nicest restaurants in town."

"Yeah, they were pretty nice," Dwight agreed. "I'll bet we end up buying our house from them too."

Willingness to meet the needs of others is what makes any cooperative relationship work. Instead of thinking only of what would be easiest, the people of one real estate firm went out of their way to meet the needs of a stranger.

If that kind of thinking makes good business sense, it surely makes good sense in relationships. As we read in Proverbs 11:24-25, "One man gives freely, yet gains even more; another withholds unduly, but comes to poverty. A generous man will prosper; he who refreshes others will himself be refreshed."

Mutual Trust and Respect

A standard characteristic of cooperative relationships is mutual trust and respect. Walter, of whom we spoke earlier, lost his trust and respect for others because he felt used. Conversely, because he was known as a man who served others, he was a highly trusted and respected individual.

If we don't emphasize ourselves, if we maintain common goals with others, and if we serve others' needs, an automatic reaction takes place. Others have respect for us. They trust us. In a cooperative relationship, each person is meeting the needs of the other, so trust and respect grows in both persons.

One of the nicest things we can hear about ourselves is, "I trust you." When people say that, it means our reactions and motivations seem good. We are apparently not operating on a set of self-serving goals.

Trust and respect are essential to all cooperation style relationships, but these attitudes are earned and do not exist until they are created.

In labor/management relationships, lack of trust and respect is one of the major problems a company can encounter. Since labor and management often adopt an adversary rather than a cooperative attitude, they frequently lack mutual trust and respect.

In newlywed relationships, by contrast, partners usually have a high degree of trust and respect, because each person is eagerly giving his or her attention to the needs of the other.

However much or little mutual trust and respect there may be in a relationship, the way to increase it is by demonstrating loyalty. The more I am convinced of your loyalty and faithfulness to me, the more I feel I can trust and respect you.

Not long ago, Carl, a friend of mine who is very loyal and faithful in his work, called me and said he was expecting to be fired from his job.

The company office he controlled was in the red, and he told me he would probably be needing a job soon because his boss wanted to see him right away.

"It can only mean the end for me," he said. "I've not been turning out the kind of work I want, and it shows. The ax is sure to fall."

A few days later Carl called and told me to forget about looking for a job for him.

"You found one?" I asked.

"No," he said, elated, "I didn't get fired! It was just the opposite. My boss called me into his office and praised me!"

The boss told Carl that even though he was having a bad year, he shouldn't get frustrated and upset with the figures and lose heart.

"I know you can pull this out," his boss told him. "I put you in charge of this division because you're the best manager I have. Just remember that I have faith in you to do it."

The next year, Carl's division produced the largest profits of any in the company. Though Carl had not succeeded one year, his boss hung in there, keeping the cooperative relationship active and alive. In relationships, trust promotes trust, and respect promotes respect. Carl speaks very highly of his boss now, and strives to be the kind of man his boss believes he is.

The loyalty that produces trust and respect is a rare attribute in modern relationships. It's even rare in our churches. Recently, a pastor of a large church on the West Coast said to me, "Loyalty is becoming a thing of the past. Many of our people have the attitude typical of society today. 'If you don't put on a good show for me this Sunday, I can just go down the street to the church on the corner next Sunday.'"

Businesses, marriages, and friendships all may find loyalty lacking. One of my neighbors, a newlywed for the third time, made a bad joke about his new marriage. "I decided to give it another try," he said. "If it doesn't work out this time, I'll have to settle for a live-in girlfriend."

Without trust built on loyalty, no relationship can prosper.

This man had little experience with either loyalty or trust, meaning his prospects of doing better are dismal.

But there are many positive examples of this principle of loyalty building trust too. Not long ago, I did a management seminar for a mining company. Mining, as you can imagine, is dangerous work. The men and women too who go down hundreds of feet into the earth must rely heavily on each other to make their work safe.

If the boss makes the wrong decision, letting safety slip, lives can be lost quickly. So workers and their bosses must have a good deal of trust and respect for each other to work under such dangerous conditions.

One afternoon, a miner came to me and told me he had a tremendous amount of trust in and respect for his boss.

"But there's a reason," he said.

It seems that one day down in the mine, his boss was working everyone extra hard and they were grumbling and getting tired. Just as they were about to quit, they accidentally stumbled onto some poison gas in one of the tunnels.

Immediately they backed off and started running for a safer area and air they could breathe. In the rush, one of the men fell and broke a leg.

"You can imagine the confusion," the young man explained to me. "Here we were, all scramblin' to get out of there, and this guy goes down. Well, none of us stopped. We just kept going, expecting somebody else to help him out."

That somebody ended up being the boss. A few moments after the men were clear of the area, they saw that neither the boss nor the injured man were with the rest of the crew.

"Before long, here he comes, carrying the man with the broken leg," the young man said. "He jumped ten notches in my respect column right there, even if he does seem rough on us sometimes."

Creativity
Everybody has his own talents and insights into life. But for most of us, if you add up all we do, our creativity certainly

isn't tapped often enough. Scientific studies show that probably a mere ten percent of our brain cells are used at any given time.

That means extra achievement from any one of us is just waiting for the proper motivation to send us digging deep into our reservoirs of experience and knowledge.

In cooperation relationships, you will see this extra effort taking place all the time. People are encouraged to use their skills, abilities, thoughts, and creativity in a cooperative setting. And they are rewarded for doing so.

Only in cooperative relationships do we draw creativity out of others. In the other three relationship styles, we try to force our ideas and suggestions on eveyone else. We want our own needs met at others' expense.

Two people's minds working together can be much more creative and productive than they can working alone. For example, for the past two years I have been trying to figure out how to landscape a steep hill in our backyard. I thought about planting grass on it, but it would be too difficult to mow. I even considered covering it with rock, just to cover up the dirt.

One day Lorraine asked me if I thought a garden would grow on the hill. I assured her the hill was too steep for a garden. We began brainstorming ideas on what to do with the hill.

I said we should have something that required little maintenance, and she said she wanted something different but attractive.

Jokingly I said, "As steep as the hill is, we should call our backyard Pikes Peak."

Her face lit up and she said, "That's it, Myron. Why don't we go to the mountains and get wild plants, trees, and shrubs and make it into a natural landscape."

We agreed that was an excellent idea, and today we have twisted stumps, multi-colored rocks, all sorts of wild flowers, grass, and bushes decorating the once-barren hill in our backyard. The idea came because we both were involved in the planning. Bits and pieces of each of our ideas came together to form a better idea than either of us would have devised on our own.

In relationships, the Bible indicates that virtually anything we attempt to do unitedly can be accomplished. The classic example of people banding together to achieve a common goal is found in Genesis 11. At Babel the people were working ferverishly to build a great tower. Even though God opposed this pagan effort, He provided an everlasting clue to the power of man's creativity in working together, saying, "If as one people speaking the same language they have begun to do this, then nothing they plan to do will be impossible for them" (v. 6).

"Nothing they plan to do will be impossible for them." We have incredible power in our creative potential. In fact, God stopped the people of Babel only by making it too difficult to exchange their ideas. He confused their speech and disrupted their communication.

When we communicate and exchange ideas to the glory of God, great things can happen. Joining in our relationships, we draw out creative talents and ideas from each other. Instead of forcing our ideas on others, we work together, joined as one in our efforts.

My own studies bear out the fact that when people work cooperatively they can achieve phenomenal results. Again and again in researching companies that maintain cooperative relationships, I've seen people accomplish things together they could not even imagine doing alone.

Continued New Commitments

A cooperative relationship does not survive perpetually on the strength of an initial handshake or kiss. Since we are bound to have problems in our relationships because of our sinful natures, we must periodically reaffirm our initial commitments to meet each other's needs. Commitment was the first major feature of a cooperative relationship in our list of six such features. Now we are saying that beyond reaffirming our initial commitments, we should continue to make new commitments so that our relationships can grow stronger in the face of new problems.

Let's consider an example from a marriage relationship. Mary and George have encountered financial problems in their life together. Each time a money hassle arises, they find themselves bickering. It's not enough for Mary to tell herself that money problems shouldn't make any difference in the marriage. It's not enough for George to think, "I told her I loved her when we got married; what more does she want?"

Falling back on their original commitment to love is not going to solve this couple's money problems. Mary and George must work together, making new commitments that strengthen their love. For instance, George might need to put in some extra hours at work, or do more around home so that Mary can go to work. That takes new commitments in the relationship.

Because new problems arise and situations change, new commitments are vital for a sustained cooperative relationship. These new commitments keep us directed toward meeting the other person's need.

In cooperation, we find that relationships develop as more commitments are made. New goals pop up, the partners in the relationship draw creativity from each other to reach the goals, and mutual trust and respect grows.

But there is an even more important aspect to new commitment. We end up solving problems together, and we have "ownership" in the solutions.

Ownership in solutions gets us emotionally involved. We are committed to what we own. In relationships, ownership is essential for us to feel like full participants. When our input and ideas contribute to more commitments, we are aware all the time of the investment we have made.

Suppose I'm having a discipline problem with my son Ron. If I say, "Here's what we're going to do," I'm probably in for some resistance. He has no personal commitment or ownership in the solution, because I'm forcing it on him.

Instead, I should approach Ron with concern for his needs and involve him in any new commitments of our relationship. "OK, Ron, what are we going to do about this?" If he is directly involved in a solution, he will own it.

When my daughter Delphine first started dating, I was trying to be an understanding parent. I told her, "Delphine, I'm going to trust you. Your mother said she would, and so will I. But I want you in by 10 P.M."

That worked out fine. She knew what she was supposed to do, and did it. For about three dates. Then she came in at 1 A.M. from a date. Lorraine and I were nervous wrecks. Fortunately, while we were waiting, we agreed not to get upset. We were going to let Delphine explain herself. Then we were going to get upset!

When Delphine came home, our patience paid off. She came in the door and started apologizing right away. She said she knew we were upset and that a punishment was necessary for what she did.

Lorraine and I looked at each other, and I turned and asked Delphine what she thought was a fair punishment.

"If I were you, I'd ground me for a month," she said.

I was thinking two weeks would be a just punishment, but I didn't balk. "All right, Delphine, a month it is." We kissed her, and we all went quietly to bed.

For the next month, Delphine never squawked once about being grounded. She owned the punishment.

Cooperative relationships allow this kind of creative, respectful, and commitment-based atmosphere to develop. But none of us are able to maintain the perfect cooperative relationship. From time to time, we forget to meet the needs of others and start thinking of ourselves.

Our partners also get worried about their needs and begin focusing on themselves. The cooperative relationship begins to change.

4

Retaliation: Moving Away from a Cooperative Relationship

The first move away from a cooperative relationship is usually subtle. It happens unconsciously. Our needs surface for a moment, and we lightly step away from cooperation, switching our emphasis from the other to ourselves.

The shift always begins covertly—without our really knowing what's happening. We might feel worried about our needs getting met, or we revel a bit too much in how wonderful it is when they are.

In either case, we stop thinking about meeting the needs of our partner. We violate the principle: "Look not only to your own interests, but also to the interests of others" (Phil. 2:4).

This threatens the other person in our relationship, and he or she may retaliate at our selfishness.

We usually deceive ourselves when we think that meeting our own need at a certain moment is more important than meeting another person's need. I've already said this several times, but I can't say it enough: *Meeting other people's needs in a cooperative style relationship is the only way to get your needs met.*

Our Perceptions Are Real
Because we are human, our perceptions about our needs are very real and important. If we perceive that we have a need,

then we do have a need. Whether a need is real in the sense of being objectively logical does not matter. If we believe a need is real, for all practical relationship purposes it is real.

We act and react from our needs, even if we are dead wrong about them. Our emotions just don't know the difference. It's a mistake to dismiss someone with, "You don't need that." If he thinks he needs it, he will act accordingly.

Consequently, in order to keep a relationship at a cooperative level, we must meet "perceived" needs even when they seem unjustified to us. If we think our partner is wrong about a need and we don't meet that need when we could, he or she is probably going to retaliate. Then we may also retaliate with, "You're wrong. You don't need that!"

Remember, any relationship forms around needs. If a relationship is not meeting our needs, we probably will try to force it to do so. The first way we do that is by striking back, attempting to make our partner "get on the stick" and meet our needs.

If I think I have a need, and my partner isn't meeting it when he should, I'm going to be hurt. It may be true that I don't really need what I want, but if I think I do, I'm captured emotionally.

Someone may tell me, "That's not a need, Myron."

My built-in reaction is, "What do you mean? Does that mean you won't help me fill my need?"

It may sound childish, but we are all emotionally invested in our needs. If you reject me when I believe my need is unmet, I hear you telling me you aren't interested in meeting my need.

Self-Righteous

For Christians, botching up perceived needs takes on a moral perspective that can be frustrating and very harmful. With our assumptions about divine and holy lives, we tend to put down people when they express their personal needs. We get self-righteous and advise people that the needs they think they have are really expressions of selfishness.

"Oh, come on. You don't really need that. Grow up and be mature! A mature Christian doesn't worry about getting his needs met."

Heard that before? Well, it isn't entirely true. If you have a need, or even a perceived need, spirituality has nothing to do with it. The laws of relationships take over. You suffer emotionally.

We tend to counsel each other as Christians to get hold of ourselves spiritually. "You shouldn't think about yourself." But that is missing the point. In the context of relationships, perceived needs strive to be met.

Misunderstanding is the culprit here. Understanding admits that the other is feeling something real, even though we do not perceive that need. To claim a person does not know what he is feeling is to misunderstand what needs are.

We have needs, perceived or real, and we must work in our relationships to meet them by meeting the needs of others. If either one of us backs off because we think the other person doesn't have a real need, deterioration of the relationship begins.

In this chapter, we'll discuss what the first subtle steps away from cooperation do to a relationship. We'll see that when we assume our partners don't really have a need they are expressing, we make life miserable for each other.

Assume and Conform

We enter the first phase in the retaliation style relationship when we believe a need of ours is not going to be met. Our reaction is to make sure the other gets going to meet that need.

"My wife has to let me watch football on Monday nights."

"My boss has got to give me a bigger office."

These and similar statements don't say *how* this will happen, but the assumption is that a need is not getting met, and we must take steps to get our partner to conform in meeting that need.

We are all this way. We make assumptions about many

things, and can easily justify making an assumption about our needs when we start to get worried about them. We make the subtle shift from *trusting* that our needs will be met to *insisting* that they be met.

It is appropriate to communicate what our needs are so that our partner can meet them. However, in retaliation we go *beyond* communicating needs, or we act *instead* of communicating needs. We feel we must do something and what we do is to demand somehow that our partner accommodate our need.

For instance, sometimes we feel we don't get enough recognition for the things we do. We lose trust, feeling that others are not giving us pats on the back as they should.

One reaction is to vocalize our need in a positive but indirect manner. "Hey, I did a good job, didn't I?"

Most of the time this works. Our partner "hears" our need coming through, agrees with us, and satisfies our need. Some times, however, a person may respond with a wisecrack or even disagree that we did a commendable job.

Our unsatisfied need won't go away, so we may get more creative in seeking recognition. We may go to someone else to praise us, or work harder the next time to "show them." If we feel ignored, we may try to make people feel guilty.

Attempts of this kind to get recognition may be skipped altogether. Some people simply "keep score" of the times they are mistreated. They don't feel free to trust others to meet their needs anymore, and even assume people will automatically forget.

We have one television set at our house. What we watch can quickly become a big family issue. One evening, Ron told the family that he needed to reserve 8-10 P.M. on a specific Tuesday night to watch a big hockey game. He wanted us all to be informed "way ahead of time," so there wouldn't be any last minute arguments.

"Yeah, OK," we all assured him, and didn't think much more about it.

However, when the Tuesday arrived, Delphine came home

from school and calmly informed the family at dinner that she had an important English assignment for the next day. She needed to watch a television special that started at 8 P.M.

Ron raised his eyebrows when Lorraine and I didn't respond. We had totally forgotten about his appointment with the hockey game, and we were just nodding our approval to Delphine.

"Oh, no, you're not, Delphine!" he said coldly. "I'm going to watch my hockey game. Remember?"

Lorraine and I remembered, and changed our nodding approval to Ron.

Delphine assumed her TV time was now in jeopardy, and she was upset that we would honor Ron's two-week old request over something so important as a class assignment. She expressed her dissatisfaction with the appointment approach to using the televison set, and proceeded to make Ron feel guilty about making her miss her program.

"I'm going to be graded, Ron," she said. "This is not just a recreational thing. I have to watch that program."

Lorraine and I stopped our nodding to consider Delphine's reasoning. Ron began to feel that the criteria of appointment-setting was not decisive in our eyes. Grades, school, and more serious consequences were at stake here. I watched the wheels turn in his head.

"Look, Delphine, I really have to watch this game," he said. "You know I'm applying for a hockey scholarship. These are two of the best teams in the country playing tonight, and I can really learn a lot about form and technique. This is going to help me get into college, because grades alone aren't going to pay for my college education."

His response was classic. He was playing one-upmanship, and trying to get Delphine to conform to his need. He had retaliated.

Both Delphine and Ron wanted the other to feel guilty about not meeting the other's need. That's usually the way we start in a retaliatory relationship. We describe our need in such a way that we become personally justified in our action of retaliation. Therefore, if the one person disagrees with meeting our need, he is guilty of mistreating us.

In this situation, we want nothing else but to win the argument. We want to hear, "Of course, you're right. Why should I have questioned?"

If this imputing guilt approach doesn't work we may take open and aggressive action—the second phase of retaliation.

Aggression

In the first phase of retaliation, when we make assumptions and nimbly attempt to get our partner to conform, there is a low level of emotion.

Throughout the next phase, aggression, we usually remain on a verbal level, but we begin to express our emotions a little more. Emotional levels are different for every person. However, when we begin to think of ourselves, we generally tend to use our emotions for effect.

Soon after Ron's claim that his college career could depend on watching a hockey game on television, he and Delphine began to argue with their emotions. Hurt looks, angry eyes, and desperate gestures are all emotional ways of making a point.

But emotional tactics don't always succeed. In such cases, we may become even more serious about getting our need met and go on the offensive. Delphine, for instance, gave up discussing which need was more important in the television debate. Instead, she launched a new aggressive attack by appealing to Lorraine and me as outside authorities who could step in. She attacked Ron through us.

"Ron always gets to watch what he wants," she told us. "It's not right that you show favoritism."

When we start aggressive verbal attacks, we tend to draw on any resource available to retaliate. Often we use past actions or similar circumstances to "prove" that we are being treated poorly. Any previous unmet need can be used as a club in our offensive attack.

"This is the fourth time this week," or "You don't let me do anything I want to do," we say.

We may go back to situations that existed years ago, even though entire relationships have changed. "I'll bet you didn't treat your little sisters that way when you were a child!"

If the past doesn't help us, we can use many other devices. One popular approach is to corral peer support, applying pressure with a third party.

Usually, third parties are "neutral" people. That is, they could be described as neutral, though they really aren't. In truth, we only pick third parties we believe will agree with us, someone to buttress our side of the issue.

For instance, a wife might call on her mother in attacking her husband. The man might call on his best friend. "Let's see what Jim thinks about this!"

In aggressive retaliation, we don't think about the other person's needs. Calling on our own "troops" to help us out is one of the telltale signs that we are thinking of ourselves.

When the verbal attack begins, the partner can do one of two things: He or she can go on the defensive, or counterattack.

In either case, an argument is going to take place. But all the argument really accomplishes is to clarify that both people are right. At that stage, no one wins. We merely confirm in our own minds that we are being challenged unjustly by someone who is unreasonable.

How we handle the aggression phase of retaliation can determine the future direction a relationship takes. Because our aggressive action is obvious, we usually aren't confused—we aren't subtly thinking of ourselves without realizing it. No, it may be unclear exactly why we are arguing, but we know we are arguing and openly favoring our own needs over the needs of others.

Underneath the emotion and harsh words, we still care deeply about the needs of our partner. In this early stage of retaliation, the relationship is still healthy. In fact, many of us find aggressive retaliation an important way to express feelings we've been keeping inside. Once our emotions have been released, we can quickly make up.

The danger in the aggression phase comes from concentrating on the emotional dialogue and purposely burying our concern for the other person because we are "fed up," or experience some other selfish feeling.

In arguments, it's as if we jump into wet cement, sort of glomping around in the muck and warning our partners that we are seriously injured by his treatment. The trouble is that while we stomp around, arguing and taking the offensive, the cement may dry, trapping us in our own ill·feelings.

Our own needs swell in importance when we are injured in an argument. Our partner takes on a different shape in our eyes. He or she is no longer the person we joined with in meeting complementary needs. Such a partner is a source of pain and injury, an object in the way of meeting our needs.

Though we are still deeply concerned about the other person's needs at this stage, we put them on the back burner to get our current needs met. Our partner's needs are now less important than our needs.

The Battle To Win

When we believe the only way to meet our own needs is by taking aggressive action, we operate under new principles. These are not principles of cooperation but principles of domination, though we have not yet entered the domination style of relating.

For every principle of cooperation, there is an opposite principle of domination. We don't actually dominate another in retaliatory relationships. We just want to win and get our needs met.

We feel we are being wronged, and therefore have no need to look out for the other person. We tend to repay evil for evil. Yet Scripture says, "Do not repay anyone evil for evil. Be careful to do what is right in the eyes of everybody" (Rom. 12:17).

To get our needs met through control, we use the kind of selfish, me-oriented thinking typical of the dominator. However, our major mistake in grasping for control is that we no longer see our partners as a person.

Very often, we don't realize that our partner might fight back, not wanting to be controlled. The surprise sometimes shocks us into apologizing.

We might be used to counterattacks. We might even be prepared for them, with plans to thwart such responses. If we stay in a retaliatory frame of mind long enough, our partner can become the perfect "enemy." We completely bury any concern we have for him or her and lock our minds.

"This time, I'm going to win," we tell ourselves.

With retaliation in full swing, our goals change. We no longer want to meet each other's needs. We want our own needs met. If reasoning, guilt trips, emotional and verbal attacks don't work, we act on principles of domination. By acting on these principles, we shove the relationship into a dangerous situation of winner and loser.

Perpetual Conflict—Five Minutes or Five Years

The partners in a retaliatory relationship sooner or later realize that domination is the name of the game. If both partners want to play the game, retaliation can go on indefinitely.

Depending on the temperament of the individuals involved, retaliation could last five minutes or five years. Some relationships never leave this phase. Are there friends you always end up in arguments with, or relatives who battle with you at every meeting? You have a retaliation style relationship.

Most of the time someone is going to emerge the winner. You've seen office situations where people don't get along. After a while a decisive battle takes place between them.

I observed such a sequence of events one day while waiting for someone in a doorway. A foreman was asking for opinions on where to put an office door. Everyone in the room seemed to have a different idea. He calmly listened to everyone, then said, "I think I'll do it my way."

One of the people in the office jumped in immediately. "I

think my idea is better than that."

"I'm the foreman here, and I've got more experience," he replied. "We do it my way."

"Then why did you ask for my opinion?" the worker almost shouted back.

"You didn't offer anything new," the foreman said coldly.

"You just don't want to hear anything new."

"That'll be enough," the foreman said, pointing his finger.

"Anything you say," the worker gruffly replied, and the retaliation was over. They were into domination, and the worker had lost the battle.

Lorraine and I experienced years of retaliatory arguments before I started to see her as an object in my way. When my opportunity to move to Alaska came up, six weeks passed before I finally dominated the situation.

When we moved the family to Alaska, I was in control and no longer interested in retaliatory approaches. Because I was the winner, I acted like it, and moved our marriage relationship into the domination style.

In retaliation, someone usually gives up eventually. But that does not settle problems. It just moves the relationship deeper into degeneration.

Never Pay Evil with Evil

Paul wrote some compelling words about retaliatory relationship styles. "Do not repay anyone evil for evil. Be careful to do what is right in the sight of everybody. If it is possible, as far as it depends on you, live at peace with everyone. Do not take revenge, my friends, but leave room for God's wrath, for it is written: 'It is mine to avenge, I will repay,' says the Lord. On the contrary: 'If your enemy is hungry, feed him; if he is thirsty, give him something to drink. In doing this, you will heap burning coals on his head'" (Rom. 12:17-20).

When our partners come at us like gangbusters, intent on controlling us to fill their needs, what should we do? Paul says, first, don't retaliate. Second, keep right on meeting the needs of the other, even though you are being mistreated.

The aggressor will always be guilty of wrongdoing. It takes a strong-willed decision on our part to hang in there and not strike back. We tend to hurt others when they hurt us. At best, many of us only wait to regroup, and plan our counterattack.

In the Sermon on the Mount, Jesus took issue with the old idea of an eye for an eye and a tooth for a tooth. He offered something new.

I tell you, Do not resist an evil person. If someone strikes you on the right cheek, turn to him the other also. And if someone wants to sue you and take your tunic, let him have your cloak as well. If someone forces you to go one mile, go with him two miles. Give to the one who asks you, and do not turn away from the one who wants to borrow from you.

You have heard that it was said, "Love your neighbor, and hate your enemy." But I tell you, Love your enemies, and pray for those who persecute you, that you may be sons of your Father in heaven. He causes His sun to rise on the evil and the good, and sends rain on the righteous and the unrighteous (Matt. 5:39-45).

In relationships, we should not allow our human nature to trip us. We must not lose sight of cooperation. Jesus plainly tells us not to let our commitment be conditioned on how we are treated.

Covert and Unconscious

Moving from cooperation to retaliation can take place without our even knowing it. We don't just hop from one to the other. When we first begin to shift, we are still concerned with meeting each other's needs. It's not until we decide that our need is more important, and take aggressive action, that we actually put our relationship on the line.

Maybe we're afraid the other person is not acting fast enough, or we are too eager to get our needs met. In any case, our shift to ourselves is usually covert and unconscious.

The prime requisite for healthy return to cooperation at this point is communication. (We will deal at length with communication in chapters 10 and 11.) The key to maintaining cooperative relationships is the willingness to openly communicate all our needs. By verbalizing our needs in a positive manner, we can forestall aggressive responses.

A phrase that Lorraine and I use to communicate under these circumstances is: When _____ occurs, I feel _____, because _____.

That little fill-in-the-blanks formula identifies our feelings and the reasons for the feelings. Things brought into the open this way can then be dealt with.

Over the years, a number of couples have come to me for counseling. Almost invariably, their marriage problems center on a need one has that the other doesn't know about or doesn't understand. If we don't say what our needs are, we can't expect to get them met. The early phases of retaliation may also flush needs out, but relying on such conflict to solve our relationship problems can eventually destroy a relationship. We must learn to communicate more positively.

Real and Perceived

I mentioned in the beginning of this chapter that many people have needs that seem unreal. Let me offer what hundreds of studies in business have shown about our inability to know other people's needs better than they do.

"What do you perceive the top ten needs of your employees to be?" That question almost always gets the same answer. Employers believe their employees want money.

But when employees list their top ten needs, money ends up at the bottom of the list. The first need that employees list is "personal job satisfaction and fulfillment."

Managers expect their employees to put personal satisfaction and fulfillment at the bottom of the list.

In any relationship, we may get high notions about our understanding of what our partners need. We see they don't "really" need what they think they do, and we don't value their perception of the need enough to meet the need.

The perceived needs of your relationship partner must be met. The way to respond to a need that doesn't seem real to you is to fill it. You may be shocked to discover that the "perceived" need is very real.

This principle is one counselors should remember too. Not long ago I was in Chicago leading a seminar with thirty Christian leaders. We were discussing the various relationship styles, and how all relationships evolve around meeting perceived needs.

At the end of the session, a pastor told me this would revolutionize his whole approach to counseling. "I can see the validity of providing what a person thinks he needs," he said. "Regardless of what I may think is perceived or real, people have needs that must be met."

Our Assumptions

We assume too many things about our relationships, and one of the worst assumptions is that our needs will not be met. If we don't talk out our concerns, we can easily slip into a pattern of thought that puts us on the track to self-centeredness.

Then we talk all right, but instead of talking about our needs in a positive and constructive manner we verbally attack the other person. We say unkind things, or provoke guilt, or even denounce our partner.

The Bible says, "He who guards his lips guards his soul, but he who speaks rashly will come to ruin" (Prov. 13:3).

When we make assumptions and let our unguarded lips speak, we are likely to put our relationships into a retaliatory phase. When we go one step further and take aggressive action because we are misled by what our own mouths are saying, we can worsen and move into domination. As we read in Proverbs 10:19, "When words are many, sin is not absent, but he who holds his tongue is wise."

The Bible describes selfishness as sin. When we worry about our own needs getting met and lose sight of our commitments to one another, we are sinning. Our needs, whether perceived or real, must be met. But failing to communicate them and then seeking control over our relationship partners is not the way.

The classic example of avoiding a move into retaliation is found in Genesis 13. Abraham and Lot experience a relationship crisis that could result in Lot's disgrace. But instead of retaliating, Abraham responds with exactly what Lot needs.

In this account, a conflict develops over sheepherders, grassland, and water. Abraham finally speaks up when the herdsmen began fighting over their "rights."

"Let's not have any quarrelling between you and me, or between your herdsmen and mine, for we are brothers," he says (v. 8). Then he asks if the whole land is not before them, and tells Lot to separate from Abraham's clan.

Lot now looks over the land from a hill, surveying the beautiful Jordan Valley with its well-watered gardens. He looks to the sides and sees the dry hills. Lot decides that he wants the valley, the entire thing. Abraham can have the scrubby land of Canaan.

Now, Abraham could wipe out Lot right on the spot. Here is this upstart, whom Abraham brought along with him and gave great privilege, asking for the prime land.

But Abraham just smiles and says, "Fine."

Abraham was committed to meeting Lot's need, real or perceived. And God honored Abraham for his deed. After Lot's departure God said to Abraham, "Lift up your eyes from where you are and look north and south, east and west. All the land that you see, I will give to you and your offspring forever" (vv. 14-15).

Abraham ended up as the father of a people who number as the dust of the earth. Lot received his need, and God honored Abraham's cooperative spirit: his refusal to assume that his needs would be unmet and his commitment to meet others' needs first.

5

Domination: The Worst Way to Relate

"Again I looked and saw all the oppression that was taking place under the sun: I saw the tears of the oppressed—and they have no comforter; power was on the side of their oppressors—and they have no comforter" (Ecc. 4:1).

In the Bible, oppression and domination receive strong condemnation. We get the impression that God judges this relationship style to be the worst we can choose.

In domination, one person is oppressed by another. All of us recognize immediately that those being dominated are in a difficult situation. They have nowhere to go. They can't go to the dominator because he won't help. They can't go to anyone else because the dominator won't let them. Consequently, the oppressed feel they have nobody to understand their needs, help them, or listen to them.

But the Bible says the dominator fares no better. There is no one to comfort him either. The dominator has power, but he is not getting what he needs.

When the domination style begins, the dominator feels justified in getting his needs met by force. He feels he has a right and deserves to dominate. But once the relationship gets going in a domination style, the dominator realizes his needs still are not being met.

He has power but no one to comfort him. His satisfaction is hollow, short-lived.

Scripture describes how awful a domination style is. "And I declared that the dead, who had already died, are happier than the living, who are still alive" (Ecc. 4: 2). It seems better to be dead than to be either a dominator or a dominated person.

"But better than both is he who has not yet been, who has not seen the evil that is done under the sun" (v. 3).

The most fortunate person is the one who never has faced this evil of domination. To say that we would be better off never having lived than even just to "see" this evil is strong language. What we do as dominators must be extremely bad.

In this chapter, we will consider how awful domination is. We will examine our characteristics when we operate as dominators and as the dominated.

Our Own Needs: All That Is Left
When I stop considering the needs of others, only one person is left. I focus on myself and my needs. In doing so, I lose all perspective. Meeting my own needs is the only important consideration, and I must never be denied.

When I was trading blows with Lorraine within the retaliation relationship we endured for so many years, I got into a habit of fighting for my needs. Therefore, it was easy for me to believe my need to move to Alaska was more important than anything else. In my mind, moving was the only logical thing to do.

My career was at stake, and my reputation was on the line. As I became more and more self-centered, I felt sure I had a "right" to go to Alaska. The next conclusion was that Lorraine did not have a right to stand in my way.

As Christians, when we begin to think like this about our "rights" in a relationship, we tend to get into mental conversations with God over who is in the wrong. We convince ourselves that God would judge us in the right, and our partner in the wrong.

This is one reason God condemns domination relationships. God does not condemn domination because we are in error about who is right and who is wrong. God condemns domination because the dominator sets himself up as the final authority, as the judge. The judge then decides whose need is more deserving. God already made that judgment before the needs even came up. God said others' needs come first. If I assume a position to veto your need, promoting my need instead, then I play God.

One Plays God, the Other Becomes Servant

In a domination relationship style, the person being dominated actually becomes the servant of the dominator. Instead of a mutual meeting of needs, the person who has the power uses it to force the other person to serve his needs.

We saw earlier in Philippians 2:3-4 that we are to do nothing from selfishness or conceit, but rather to count others better than ourselves. We do just the opposite in domination. We operate out of selfishness, and set ourselves up as more important.

As children, most of us experienced the domination of older brothers and sisters over younger ones. I know I certainly did.

Norma is my older sister by six years. When we were growing up, we would play well together until one of her friends came over. Immediately, my sister would have nothing to do with me, and start playing with her friend. When I would approach them wanting to play too, they would chase me off.

Being older, my sister was in a position to dominate me easily. When her friends came over to play, she had no concern for my needs. If I was too persistent, she would go to Mother and tell on me. Almost always, I was told to leave the girls alone and let them play.

"Mother, I have a right to play with my own friends," my sister used to say.

Sometimes I was able to play with Norma and her friends, but only if they needed me to get the bicycles, move the furniture, or do some other chore. When they were through with me and I wouldn't leave, they just changed games. Then I would be a bother again, and in the wrong.

Being younger meant I was weaker and subject to domination. I had to play whatever game my sister and her friend wanted to play, and live by their ground rules, or be out of the picture. "Myron, we'll let you play, if...." Then a set of conditions would follow.

A few years after I was born, my parents had another child, Judy. She was the third in line. I had the opportunity as she grew up to be the dominator in our relationship. Age meant power, and age now was on my side.

By this time, Norma was almost grown, and seldom around for child's play. I was the one who took charge. As Judy grew up, I made her play basketball and football with me. Those were the games I liked.

When she wanted to play games she liked, I said, "I'll play with you if you'll play with me first." I decided the ground rules, and my little sister had to serve me.

This practice of setting ground rules creates an oppressive environment for the one being dominated. Dominated people have to come to the dominator for approval, checking in to see if whatever they want to do is OK. Eventually, they find themselves being forced to do only those things approved by the dominator.

Once I learned that model of operating as a child, I played it out in my marriage. I learned in growing up with my sisters that the people who have power to make decisions are the ones who get to do what they want.

It was easy for me to unconsciously make the decision to gain power over Lorraine so I could move the family to Alaska, because I learned as a child that power meant you got your own way.

Do What You Want, and the Other Loses Freedom

As the person with power dominates, the other person is suffocated, and no longer has the freedom to be himself.

Scripture teaches that people in a position of power should

not use that power to their own personal advantage: "We who are strong ought to bear with the failings of the weak, and not to please ourselves. Each of us should please his neighbor for his good, to build him up" (Rom. 15:1-2).

The difficult thing about applying this is that once we get power, we tend by nature to use that power for our own benefit. When we are dominating and controlling others, we will use that power in any way we can to get our own needs met in the relationship.

The above passage says we should use power to meet others' needs. Instead we get this uncontrollable urge to stamp out failure and weakness in others. We criticize, condemn, and try our best to force weakness out of existence.

Power is for building up others. Power is to be given away. When we give power to others in our relationships, they no longer are weak failures. However, it is extremely difficult for us to give away power because we think we can do a better job of removing weakness and failure from others than they can. We also don't want to give up power because we are somewhat weak and insecure within.

But that's the biblical message. Give your power away so that other people can be like you. Live in a cooperative style, meeting one another's needs.

When we violate this principle of giving away power, we become buried deeper in the mire of a domination relationship. This prevents our partner from being all he should be individually.

A friend of mine serves as pastor in a large church. His position as senior pastor elevates him to the top leadership role, giving him more power at his disposal than the rest of the staff.

His job description assigns him more decision-making power and more responsibilities. Recently, a disagreement developed between him and his minister of music over the type of music to emphasize in the church.

During their discussion, the senior pastor finally admitted he was actually trying to impose his own personal preference and tastes on the congregation. The consensus of the people and the advice of the music minister didn't matter to him.

He ended up forcing the minister of music to disregard his own professional background and to adopt a style of music that suited the taste of the one in power, namely the pastor.

The minister of music found out in a cruel, abrupt manner that he was not free to use his own judgment about something he was hired to do. Instead, he had to serve the needs of the person in power, who was abusing his own powerful situation as senior pastor.

Everyone Loses Respect

If domination is allowed to continue, eventually people will lose respect for each other. When this happens, each begins focusing on the negative and weak side of the other. Criticism builds on both sides of the domination fence. The dominator is disgusted with the dominated, and the dominated condemns the actions of the dominator.

Several years ago when managing a large federal project, I hired Sue, a psychologist friend of mine, to develop the counseling division.

Sue was recognized as a leading expert in her field of higher education. Shortly after joining my staff, she married Ed, a schoolteacher. Within a short time, their relationship began to focus on who was the superior person.

Sue had more education than Ed, and she began using that as a club in arguments. She was also teaching and operating at the university level, while her husband was teaching and operating at the elementary school level.

Sue had a strong personality, which was one of the reasons I hired her for the difficult position of running a counseling department. But that power of personality went to her head. In a subtle way, she boasted at work about how she was the boss in her marriage. When there was a fight, she won it. Eventually, Sue gained control of the marriage. It was a challenge to her, and she felt driven to dominate Ed.

Ultimately, Sue was making the decisions on the house they

purchased, the new car they selected, the type of friends they cultivated, and even how they spent their free time. She loved tennis, and literally forced Ed to take up the sport. She was a good and practiced tennis player, and consequently was superior in the sport. She even proceeded to tease Ed and let him know he was not quite the athlete she was.

A year after they were married, Ed had an opportunity to go on to graduate school to further his education. He was struggling with his decision, and couldn't make up his mind. He told me he liked the classroom and didn't want to end up in administration with a desk job and no students.

One day, Sue walked into my office, furious with Ed. She closed the door and complained to me that Ed kept asking her what he should do about graduate school. She said she couldn't respect a man unable to make up his own mind; it meant he was weak.

The irony of the whole situation was that she had virtually required Ed to act like this, to get her approval on everything he did. He was so dominated by Sue that he didn't feel that he could act without her permission.

Ed told me the same thing sometime later when we met and the subject came up. He realized that the reason he couldn't make a decision was because Sue had to approve what he did. She was calling him weak, and Ed said he was just doing what he thought she wanted in the relationship.

One day Ed and I went fishing, and all day long he criticised Sue. He complained to me what a self-centered wife Sue was, and how she constantly forced him to be the kind of person she thought she deserved for a husband.

Ed admitted to me that he had lost all respect for Sue (which is just what she had said about him). "All of her degrees in psychology certainly have not helped her learn how to be a wife," he said. A few months after that fishing trip, Sue and Ed were divorced.

Just as domination leads to loss of respect, so lack of respect breeds more domination. When Sue lost respect for Ed, she treated him worse than she probably ever imagined she could.

When we find opportunities to renew respect in our relationships, we should jump at the chance. Because the more we lose respect for each other, the more we destroy the individuality of the one we dominate.

A Slave Has No Creative Outlet

Eventually, a person being dominated finds no opportunity for personal creativity. Life is reduced to conformity.

People involved in such a relationship become inundated with rules and regulations. The one being dominated finds himself conforming to several lists of dos and don'ts, wills and won'ts. The dominator finds himself making up these incredibly time-consuming and taxing lists, and policing his partner to see that the rules are being obeyed.

When I was dominating Lorraine, the situation degenerated to the point where she had to check with me before she could even plan a menu. This included parties, evenings out, and what food we would take to a potluck.

Meal preparation was something Lorraine had enjoyed. During our retaliation style relationship, meals were one thing she could handle without my interfering. When I was dominating I took control there too. Her creativity reached low ebb.

At this point, Lorraine's self-image was all but destroyed. She became a complete shadow of my desires. I liked miniskirts, so she had to wear them. I liked Mexican food, so she fixed it for me. I liked to hunt and fish, so our weekends were spent outdoors.

Taking over the meals began to be a chore for me. I would have to tell Lorraine before I went to work what I wanted for dinner. Often I would harrass her into fixing something that wasn't such a great idea. She would prepare it, and I would blame the unsatisfactory meal on her.

It is a major tragedy for a relationship when one partner solves all the problems, makes all the decisions, and comes up with all the good ideas. No matter how brilliant, clever, and wise the dominator is, the relationship will be restricted in innovative and talented use of creativity.

If the dominator doesn't have the answer in a situation, the problem simply doesn't get solved. The fantastic potential that existed when the relationship was formed is never realized.

Another debilitating effect is that the dreams of the one being dominated remain only dreams. They soon turn into hopeless fantasies, and become painful even to think about.

The dominator is not only dominating the personality, he is controlling the entire person. If something isn't his idea, it "won't work."

The dominator eventually arrives at the false conclusion that he is the only one who ever comes up with right answers, good ideas, and solutions to problems in the relationship.

When Sue began her career in Texas, she had both natural ability and an educational background in psychology to support her creative thinking. People recognized her for this talent and frequently gave her credit for good work.

After being told for a long time how intelligent she was and how good a psychologist she was, Sue began to consider herself an authority beyond criticism.

This concept of superiority affected everything she did. She believed she could do no wrong, in all areas of her life. Her concept of what a marriage should be was the right concept. Her concept of a good husband was correct, and her husband should pay whatever price was necessary to match that concept.

What Sue did—and what all of us are constantly tempted to do—is set herself up as the model for the rest of mankind. Her philosophy of marriage and her theories of life soon became the sole way she operated and demanded that others operate. She couldn't tolerate disagreement.

Today, Sue's originality and innovative approaches to psychology have gone stale. She is not the same sharp, sensitive-to-detail person she used to be. Her lack of flexibility has alienated the very ones who used to applaud her ingenuity. She is no longer a respected, creative, and sought-after person.

In my relationship with Lorraine, I couldn't tolerate disagreement either. If Lorraine didn't agree with my ideas, I verbally attacked her. "Lorraine, you shouldn't disagree with me because my ideas are superior, and here are fourteen reasons you should concur."

When I was a kid growing up with my little sister who wanted to play on the swing, I could give her many reasons it was more important to play football. I was the more creative one in the relationship.

We become either offended or surprised when those we dominate question our authority about creative aspects in the relationship. What we fail to realize is that even if I'm dominating you, your ideas still exist in your mind. You don't really believe my ideas are the best, only that I have the "right" to supercede and overrule you.

When the one being dominated finally tires of being stifled, finally wearies from giving in, and decides he must have opportunity to use his creativity, he will remove himself from the relationship.

When God created us, He made us in His image—as creative beings. We have a driving need to exercise our creativity. The development of things new and the redesigning of things old can be observed in what we do every single day.

When a family moves into a new home, they redecorate it. They relandscape the yard in some fashion, taking something from one form and changing it into another.

This changing and developing shows us and others what we are like. If we don't have this opportunity to interact creatively with something, we don't attach much value to it. If we can't fix up the yard to our liking or redecorate the house as we see fit, we will be on guard about overstepping our bounds, have diminished interest in the place, and jump at the chance to move into a house where we have more freedom.

The same is true with relationships. If there is little opportunity for creativity in a given relationship, we will jump at another relationship that does promise such opportunity.

This issue of creative opportunity or the lack of it eventually becomes the focal point in domination-ruled relationships. The issue becomes, "Who is being used?"

In a cooperative relationship, the joint creative input of the partners solves the problems that arise. Each person's contribution gives him a degree of ownership in the relationship. Since by nature we invest heavily only in those things we can consider "ours," ownership is a powerful factor in making our relationships work.

One difference between a cooperative relationship and a domination relationship is that the former involves collective ownership and the latter does not. A dominated person doesn't own anything. The dominator makes the decisions, solves the problems, and injects the ideas. The commitment level of the dominated person is extremely low because his creativity isn't used.

When we lived in Alaska, I saw in a window of a department store a coat I thought would look good on Lorraine. She didn't like the style. Even so, I bought her the coat, and insisted she wear it.

The very next fall, someone expressed interest in the coat, and Lorraine quickly gave it away. She then made it a point to pick out her own coat, and she loved it. She was really sad recently when it began to wear out.

Both coats kept her warm. In fact, I have difficulty seeing any special difference between them. But Lorraine "owned" the second coat.

Six years ago, Lorraine and I bought a new house. I arbitrarily decided that Lorraine would fix up the inside of the house, and I would fix up the outside. As a result, when we finally moved into the finished home there was a division of "ownership."

This division became the focus of continual conflict. We constantly jabbed at each other's lack of creativity, wisdom, or skill.

When water came flowing down a nearby hill into the backyard and washed out Lorraine's flower garden, she criticized me for building a retaining wall in a stupid fashion.

When it came time to replace the carpet, I criticized Lorraine for installing a low-grade, cheap carpet in the beginning. We were at each other's throats as long as we lived in that house.

Today, we live in a house we both designed. Together we landscaped a similar backyard hill. The dumb thing still washes out when the rains come, but I don't get criticized anymore. I certainly won't be criticizing Lorraine about the carpet when it comes time to replace it, because I helped select it.

The Dominated Turn to Manipulation

In a domination relationship, the dominated eventually conclude that they can no longer tolerate their stifling situation. Usually, they resort to manipulation as a last ditch effort before actually calling off the relationship.

This manipulation is the attempt to seize control of the relationship from the dominator. It can take many forms, from outright revolution to pitiful pleading.

This may seem an honorable (or at least logical) way to save a relationship, but manipulation almost always backfires. When a person resorts to manipulation, he has decided that the relationship is not "fair" anymore, and is making a last ditch effort to finally get some needs met.

But the dominator is used to being in control. Suddenly finding himself in an opposite role of being dominated, even indirectly, does not create the response for which the manipulator hopes.

The dominator usually has no reason to crumble in the face of one-time oppression. Rather, he feels justified in striking back harder than the dominated person has previously experienced. One of the first common reactions is to threaten to end the relationship right there on the spot. This is not a decision to end the relationship, only a threat.

The dominated person now feels acute defeat. Attempting to manipulate the dominator has only hastened a feeling of hopelessness. The dominated person concludes that the relationship is a lost cause.

The dominator, on the other hand, considers the dominated person's hopeless reaction as a complete win. He feels sure that the dominated one will not fight back again.

The dominated person now feels totally rejected.

Rejected and Isolated

In terms of relationship principles, it is important to recognize that the person being dominated takes the next step toward isolation.

The dominator never moves to isolation first. He may think he is making that decision, but the one being dominated has stopped all communication and responsiveness before the dominator realizes that the relationship is on its last legs.

The key to knowing that a relationship is headed for isolation is when the one being dominated begins talking with other people about manipulating the partner into "finally" meeting his or her needs.

The dominated person tells someone he can talk with that there are too many emotional pressures to continue the relationship. He feels rejected and hopeless, and he longs for a change. The dominator doesn't long for this change.

In the case of Sue and Ed described earlier, Ed began to manipulate Sue into letting him go to graduate school. He didn't feel he could just go on his own, and he wanted Sue to give her approval. Sue became incensed at Ed for even attempting such a thing with her. She began calling him names and publicly declaring him weak and spineless.

Ed was completely dejected by this, having expected a turnaround from Sue that was miles from even understanding. She had long since forgotten his personal needs, and Ed was mired in the hopelessness of trying to get them met.

At this point he simply stopped responding to her at all, and began talking to other people about how he needed to change the relationship and make Sue into the kind of wife she should be. He was totally unrealistic, and probably never approached Sue with his feelings. He tried to work it out on the side instead.

Earlier I described an evening when Lorraine played up to my every wish, trying to get me to realize that I was ruling her life. She fixed me a fine Mexican dinner, sent the kids off for the night, and even put on one of those miniskirts that she abhorred.

When we came to the romantic spot of the evening and she put on her sexiest nightgown, she dropped her last-ditch-effort bomb by saying she had a headache. She tried to manipulate me into conforming to her will.

I would have none of it. I not only didn't understand why she was acting that way but threw back a stinging response. I told her there were "plenty of other fish in the ocean" and stormed out of the house.

When we attempt futile revenge tactics, we are only eliminating some of the last opportunities we have to salvage the relationship.

In the next chapter, we'll discuss the final relationship style, in which we isolate ourselves. At that point, no excitement, creativity, or mutually satisfying cooperative relationship remains. Everything of any value to our relationships has completely faded away.

6

Isolation: Focusing
on Ourselves

How many of us have brothers and sisters, or once-close friends, with whom we haven't been on speaking terms for a long time? It happens even with marriage partners.

Perhaps you can think of at least one relationship you have that is at this stage right now.

No matter what relationship has moved into isolation, you can be sure someone in the relationship began to focus on his or her own needs and not the needs of the others in the relationship. Someone has violated Philippians 2:3-4.

A relationship can degenerate from cooperation to isolation in only five minutes. For instance, your new employer mistreats you and you immediately complain. In no time at all he wins the fight (he *is* the boss), and begins to dominate. You promptly retreat into isolation.

In other cases, reaching isolation might take five years, or longer. In any case, getting to isolation is a degenerative process that moves at first with subtleness and finally with purposeful vengeance.

But remember, before a relationship ever gets out of domination and into isolation, the person being dominated takes the initial step away from domination and into isolation. It is never the dominator.

This is important to understand if we are trying to help other people going through relationship problems. It is equally important to understand this point if we are trying to see where we are ourselves in relationships.

Three Harmful Conclusions

Dominated people make three conclusions before moving into an isolation style relationship. First, because of a feeling of rejection and self-pity, they conclude that their partner has no concern for their needs. They see the partner as a totally self-centered dominator, and no longer a partner in a relationship. They now fully believe that their own creativity, ideas, and feelings will be given no consideration.

In essence, they no longer have any identity of their own. They consider themselves outcasts and alone in their commitment and loyalty.

Second, they conclude they need no longer forgive their partners. After absorbing all the hurts that accompany a domination relationship, they feel more wronged than willing to forgive.

The self-centeredness of the dominator and his lack of concern for his partner's needs is "too much." Most of us have a built-in limit to how much we will take from dominators. If an offense is continually committed against us, we gradually lose a sense of obligation to forgive. At some point, we simply quit forgiving.

We draw the line and begin thinking it is our turn to hurt and wrong those who have hurt us. But the Bible says, "Do not say, 'I'll pay you back for this wrong!' Wait for the Lord, and He will deliver you" (Prov. 20:22).

Peter said much the same thing. "Do not repay evil with evil or insult with insult, but with blessing" (1 Peter 3:9).

When we move into an isolation relationship, we do it because we have decided it's a way to get even. The Bible makes it very clear that getting even is not the way to handle the problem of domination.

Third, dominated people eventually conclude their needs

are never going to be met. They feel hopeless. That night in our master bedroom in Alaska after Lorraine tried to manipulate me, she realized that I dominated every aspect of her life, including our sexual relationship.

At this hopeless point, the relationship changed. Lorraine was no longer just a dominated wife. She isolated herself from me, deciding to cope with the hopeless relationship in another way. She pretended I wasn't there anymore.

The first and third conclusions—that the partner doesn't care and that hope is gone—may well be the only ones a person being dominated can accept. Such a person may think he is at last coming to grips with reality. The second conclusion, however—not to forgive—is a decision that the Bible never leaves us room to make.

Matthew 18:21-22, mentioned earlier, bears repeating. Peter speaks up to Jesus about something that is bothering him. He says, "Lord, how many times shall I forgive my brother when he sins against me? Up to seven times?"

Peter expressed what many of us think, or decide for ourselves. "How long do I have to put up with being wronged by this person? Where do I draw the line and say, 'Enough'?"

At what point in time do I conclude I am justified in no longer trying to maintain the relationship? Every person arrives at that question.

Peter suggested forgiving seven times to indicate a big number. He no doubt felt quite righteous and thought seven would almost be overextending himself. "Lord, don't You think that's a lot of forgiving?"

Jesus answered with an unexpected statement that many people refuse to accept. "I tell you, not seven times, but seventy-seven times (v. 22).

Jesus knew what the result would be if He said, "Forgive them a few times and then throw in the towel." Once a person stops forgiving, there can be no hope for the relationship. It can be restored to cooperation only if we will forgive.

At the very heart of Peter's suggestion of forgiving seven times, self-centeredness lurks. Peter is already thinking only of his own needs just by asking the question.

As long as we are willing to forgive the offenses of others, there is hope in our relationships. A relationship can be rebuilt if we "forget" how many times we've been wronged, and forgive anew. When we try to keep count, we eventually stop forgiving.

That's what happened to Lorraine. She came to the conclusion that she no longer had to forgive this man to whom she was married. I had hurt her too many times. So she withdrew into isolation.

No More Dominated Aggression

When Lorraine reached the point of total hopelessness, she stopped communicating with me beyond the absolutely necessary instructions and responses of living in the same house with another person. This illustrates the first thing that happens in isolation: The dominated person mentally blocks out the dominator.

When I came home from work at night, Lorraine would busy herself with activity the minute I walked in the door. Any activity would do, so long as she could avoid dealing with me.

Psychologically, I no longer existed; Lorraine had blocked me out of her mind and escaped with her enormous burden of unmet needs. Blocking me out allowed her to survive emotionally in my presence. At this point, our relationship was, of course, almost a total wreck.

In such a deteriorated relationship, we are now beyond any type of aggression on the part of the dominated person. Aggression began diminishing back in the retaliation stage, when the now dominated person began to lose the domination battle. It ended completely with the disaster of attempted manipulation at the end of the domination relationship.

From this point on, the dominated person retreats and withdraws. Any major confrontation is avoided because the hopelessness of getting needs met is an accepted fact.

The sooner such a person, operating from weakness, arrives

at the view that it is his or her "right" not to put up with any offense, and the better he or she becomes at avoiding the dominator, the quicker the isolation process works out a total end to the relationship.

The speed of the isolation process depends on the depth of the relationship. It could be over in minutes, or it could take years.

In marriage the long process is often the case. Over a period of time, we evolve into the isolation relationship, unaware of what has taken place. We almost assume that the isolation relationship always existed, that it is the normal state.

Ignoring Physically and Mentally

We can draw a parallel between children and adults in isolation. Children learn at an early age how to operate in isolation. They are more honest about it than adults.

When our daughter Delphine was in kindergarten, she made a new friend named Mary. Every day after school, Mary was at our house or Delphine was at hers. One day, Delphine came home from school in tears. She explained that she and Mary, "her very best friend," had gotten into a fight at school.

About an hour after Delphine got home, another friend called and invited her over to play. Delphine said sure. Then she learned that Mary was there. "I can't come over as long as she's there," Delphine said.

Children openly show that they want nothing to do with a person with whom an isolation relationship exists. An adult will tolerate physical presence if necessary, and eliminate the "enemy" mentally. He could be in the same room and yet be tuned out completely.

Isolation can also be exhibited in the context of work relationships. The most common example is in planning sessions or other business meetings where an isolated leader will call for input. He will consistently find that people are unwilling to give the input he needs. They will say, "Oh, do whatever you want."

Usually, the employees or associates aren't even in tune

with what's going on. They are not willing to be a part of the decision-making process anymore. They've given up.

There isn't one issue in a job that an employee isn't concerned about. Therefore, when you hear, "Oh, do what you want," you can be sure isolation is the relationship style.

The employees have concluded that the boss or leader is a dominator and will do what he wants anyway, so why tell him what they think.

All Communication Stops
When we mentally block out others, we accelerate the decline of the relationship, because all communication stops. In due time, some important issues must be discussed. When the dominated person refuses to communicate, one of two things must happen. The dominator must either continue with a relationship that is only a formality or go out of the relationship and into another one.

When I was in graduate school at Central Mississippi State University, I had an Education Psychology professor who one day told me, "Today's my 35th wedding anniversary."

Before I could say congratulations, he added, "We haven't carried on a five-minute conversation in ten years." He just shrugged and went on his way.

Over the course of that semester, we became good friends and from time to time talked in the student lounge over coffee.

One day he told me his story. His wife had always wanted him to make a lot of money. Historically, college professors don't get rich, and for the first several years of their marriage, there was constant conflict over this issue.

He said, "Myron, about ten years ago I realized the only way to continue living with my wife was to ignore her."

He said the issue of finances surfaced even when they talked about the weather. His solution was not to talk about anything.

Whenever we stop talking about an issue in a relationship, we go straight to isolation. This doesn't necessarily mean that our entire relationship assumes the isolation style. The four styles we've described aren't water-tight compartments so that we must be altogether in one or another. We might have quite a combination of styles in a relationship.

Nevertheless, one aspect of a relationship does affect the whole relationship. All communication will eventually stop if we don't discuss and attempt to resolve conflicts, putting us completely in the isolation style.

When anything said brings up an unresolved issue between people, they need to meet that issue head on and get it settled. Relationships can fall apart over the silliest issues, because we begin to create incredible pictures of what an ogre the other person is for not meeting our needs.

A person will debate and argue before his relationship gets to isolation, but afterward he just retreats. He is no longer willing to discuss problems.

In a way, blocking out a dominator is getting back at him. It's the "silent treatment," but a dangerous method of operating. Once the dominated person takes this approach, the dominator becomes extremely frustrated and angry.

When Lorraine imposed the silent treatment on me, I began pushing sensitive subjects at her to force her out of isolation. She only said, "I don't want to talk about it."

We could sit through an entire meal in dead silence, not speaking a word. If we did talk, it was to the kids, and sometimes to each other through them. For a while, we communicated some necessary matters that kept the household operating by telling Ron or Delphine to pass the word on.

Our silence eventually frustrated me beyond control. Lorraine was becoming comfortable with our new situation, and I was going crazy. I couldn't budge her.

One evening at dinner she said to Ron, "Tell your father to pass the potatoes."

I was sitting right at the table. When she did that, I grabbed the potatoes and said, "Lorraine, I'm right here. All you have to do is ask me for the potatoes." Then I shoved the potatoes right into her face.

Had that occurred when we were operating in a retaliation relationship, Lorraine would have responded verbally and physically. However, in isolation, she was no longer willing to deal with my acts of domination and aggresssion. She quietly got up from the table and walked out of the room to clean her face.

Her mode of dealing with me had changed completely. In her retreat state, there was no communication at all. And that frustrated me completely.

Suspicion Breeds Mistrust
When communication breaks down, so does everything else. The first thing to go is trust. The mistrust in Lorraine's and my relationship skyrocketed. I couldn't trust Lorraine behind my back at home. I didn't know what she might be telling the kids.

Lorraine couldn't trust me at work. At one point, she even thought that I really did go out and find "another fish in the ocean."

Neither of us knew anymore what was going on in the other partner's mind. In such a state, we no longer discussed our needs or aired our feelings. Each of us became more and more suspicious about the actions and reactions of the other.

I didn't know how to deal with Lorraine. I began to play games to set her up for a conflict. I harassed and needled her, even in front of the kids, but I still got no response.

Since all communication had ceased between us, suspicions mounted. At one point, my secretary invited Lorraine and me over to her house for an evening. Lorraine assumed she was about to be told that the secretary and I were going to run off together.

I found that Lorraine's suspicions were goading me on. As the isolation relationship progressed, my secretary actually became more and more attractive to me. I found it easy to talk with her. Since there was no communication at home, I would find it at work.

It crossed my mind on several occasions that I'd have a far

better relationship with my secretary than with my wife. I began to realize that Lorraine and I were hitting rock bottom.

As mistrust mushrooms, we constantly guess at every action of the other person. Usually we guess the worst, and sometimes turn the unthinkable into a reality.

Problems Multiply

In the meantime, all the problems in the relationship that had brought us to isolation were still unresolved. Lorraine and I no longer communicated, and our problems became a cancer, infecting every aspect of our relationship.

In a marriage, most couples experience continual problems with finances and kids. Everything they do usually brings up some money or child-related issue.

If a married couple can't resolve these problems because they refuse to communicate their feelings and needs, they don't have much of a future. You can't escape money and child problems for long in a marriage relationship.

In employment situations, employees continually grate with employers over benefits, job assignments, and working conditions. It's inevitable, even in the best of employer/employee relations.

If the two parties can't discuss an unresolved issue in these areas, somebody is likely to quit. Or worse, the company suffers irreparable damage in some unrelated area such as customer service or product quality.

As problems remain unresolved, more problems arise.

Problems rapidly complete the downward spiral of a relationship that is unchecked in its process of isolation. The relationship bogs down in new, severe problems that hinge on problems the partners won't even talk about.

When we block each other out, avoiding conversation and communication even by body language, we leave ourselves wide open to fantasy and imaginations of further wrongdoing by our partners. Our distorted relationship not only ceases to fill already unmet needs, it creates new needs that are impossible to meet under the current circumstances.

Unmet Needs Breed More Self-Centeredness

The more unmet needs we have in our relationships, the more self-centered we become. The only way to handle this self-centeredness problem is to express our needs openly and honestly in a sincere effort to get our partners to understand them.

When I talk about this at seminars, people often tell me, "That's spiritual immaturity, to bring up your own needs."

That's simply not true. We have little control over our feelings of self-centeredness when it comes to unmet needs. We must communicate these needs to those who are committed to us to meet them. Immaturity is hiding those needs.

What about martyrdom? True martyrdom, the sainthood kind, is when we give ourselves uncondemningly. Martyrdom doesn't mean that we give ourselves without trying to communicate. The grim truth is that as long as you are human, you are going to be self-centered about your unmet needs.

It's a law of human nature as designed by God that unmet needs will arouse the same response from us as slamming a car door on a finger. It hurts!

You can't ignore your unmet needs, because they constantly get your attention. The tragedy of moving into an isolation relationship is that mentally blocking out the other only increases the number of unmet needs you must deal with.

It may seem like a great idea to stiffen up and "take it" like any good martyr would, but that's not martyrdom in the true sense. That's ignorance breeding more pain and hurt and making life more miserable for everyone involved. Eventually that false martyrdom becomes unbearable, and the real sin follows. In order to meet our own needs, we completely reject the ones we once loved.

Refusal to communicate may sound like a great idea, but it doesn't work. As unmet needs increase in an isolation relationship, all people in the relationship become more and more self-centered. This becomes a vicious circle. The more self-centered I become, the more I ignore your needs in the relationship. At this point, no one's needs are really being met.

Now Both Are in Isolation

It takes awhile before both people move into isolation. Eventually the partners are on an even keel. Just as once they shared mutual feelings of cooperation, they now share mutual feelings of isolation. Nobody dominates anymore, but nobody is doing anything for anybody either.

Everyone ends up going through the same emotional processes. The dominator realizes he is being rejected, and he begins to feel he has a "right" to end his obligations to the other. He also decides to stop forgiving, and resigns to the fate of not getting his needs met. If the relationship has lasted this long, it is for all practical purposes over.

Only one step is left: termination.

Cooperation and Isolation—a Vast Difference

Let's look again at the characteristics of a cooperation relationship. They are:

1. Commitment to continually meet the other person's needs

2. A constant focus on a common goal

3. Unselfishness

4. Development of mutual trust and respect

5. Emphasis on mutual creativity

6. Continued new commitments

What do we find in isolation style relationship? The exact opposite:

1. A retraction of commitment to meet the other person's needs.

2. No common goals. Each partner develops goals to meet his own needs, and may even reject the idea of a single goal for the partners in the relationship.

3. Selfishness, and unconcern for the other as a person. Viewing the other person only in this worst light.

4. Mistrust and disrespect, to the point of creating new problems in the relationship through suspicion and hostility.

5. No creativity in the relationship, but a harmful constricting of the partners' lives.

6. Further weakening of the relationship from continual unresolved problems, mistrust, and a growing desire to terminate the relationship.

It Doesn't Have to be this Way

We don't have to follow this dismal course in our relationships. We should realize that we will probably sometimes experience the cycle from cooperation to retaliation to domination, to isolation, and finally to termination. However, we don't have to go beyond retaliation. We can follow some clear, easily remembered biblical principles of how to relate to others and make our relationships work.

But if our relationships are to "work," we must work at them. We can't blithely exist in perpetual cooperation, resting assured in calm, loving relationships. We must work at keeping the characteristics of the cooperation relationship active in our lives all the time.

When Lorraine and I came to the extremes of isolation, we could easily have lost the most important relationship in our lives. The wonder of being able to meet each other's needs could have vanished. The excitment of creating joint goals and accomplishing great things could have died.

If that had happened, we might never have realized how to be truly unselfish and forgiving. We might never have experienced the security of being trusted and respected by someone close to us.

That's the "stuff," the meat, the purpose of relationships. It's too precious to forfeit.

Part 2
Prescription

7

How to Restore a
Relationship

In part 1 of this book, we described the style of a relationship. We considered examples of how any relationship can degenerate from cooperation to isolation. But that is not all you need to know.

Knowing how relationships fall apart does create awareness. For some, that may be such new information that they will at once begin to improve in how they operate with family, friends, and associates.

But knowing specifically what to do to keep your relationships healthy and cooperative will help you even more. The second part of this book is designed to provide you with some of that specific know-how. The six chapters are devoted to:

● The "formula" for returning a relationship to cooperation
● How to handle conflict
● Teamwork and developing common goals
● How to share your thoughts and feelings
● How to become a good listener
● Controlling your attitudes and commitments

The Back to Cooperation "Formula"
When Lorraine and I were at the end of the isolation cycle in Alaska, I tried to figure out what I should do next.

I had told Lorraine I wanted a divorce. I had told my employer I was resigning and would soon leave. That made me feel better for awhile. But the relief from blurting out my wish to escape was short-lived. I soon began to feel empty and lost.

A few days passed, and the dust began to settle. I went for a long walk in the park alone. Though the conviction to divorce Lorraine was something about which I felt strongly, I did not feel at all comfortable with the horrible mess my life was in.

I sat down on a park bench, took out a piece of paper, and wrote down the two problems that were pressing on my mind.

1. How did I get into this mess?
2. If this weren't me, what would I tell me?

As a consultant, I was used to advising others, and I soon found myself writing down some answers. The first thing I wrote was that I, Myron Rush, was going to have to admit that both Lorraine and I were responsible for this situation.

I almost got snagged right there, not wanting to completely admit my guilt. But I knew, objectively, that I must share the blame for our wrecked relationship. As I thought about it further, it seemed that all my education, Bible study, and management background would end up supporting me. But what I learned was quite the opposite. Eventually I reached conclusions that I could not deny.

I wrote down five things on my little piece of paper. I looked at those five things and told myself that implementing them was impossible. There was no way I could do them. I shoved the paper into my pocket and left the park, troubled.

The next day at work, during a lull in my day's activities, I sat thinking about the mess of my life and remembered the list I had made in the park.

I pulled it out of my jacket pocket and read my five impossibles. It was then that they struck me as clear and workable steps to restoring our relationship, even though they were stingingly painful things to do.

Here's what I had on my list:

1. Be willing to admit to yourself and others what the current situation really is (Matt. 5:23-24).

2. Admit that it is your own selfishness that led you to the relationship problem, and that selfishness is sin. Therefore, ask God and others in the relationship to forgive you, and you forgive them for their wrongdoing also (Matt. 6:14-15; Col. 3:12-13).

3. Decide to start putting the needs of the other person ahead of your own (Phil. 2:3-4).

4. Begin acting out 1 Corinthians 13:4-8, which gives a detailed description of love in action.

5. Start thanking God for the other person or persons in the relationship and their contribution to it (1 Thes. 5:18).

I knew these were sound steps, because for several years Lorraine and I had learned these things from our Bible study groups. Each step also fit my experience in management training, though I knew most management situations didn't reflect that ideology.

The genius of the ideas hit my vanity button and my fear button both at the same time. I knew in my heart and my brain that they would work, because they were based on biblical principles and commands.

Admitting the Relationship Problem Exists

We need to remind ourselves constantly that everyone experiences relationship problems. No one escapes them.

In an earlier chapter we said that Christians sometimes have a major problem admitting their relationships are troubled, especially within the home.

We too often equate relationship problems with spiritual immaturity. It has been my experience that the more people are recognized as spiritual leaders in the community, the harder it is for them to admit to relationship problems.

Admitting that you have relationship problems is not a sign of spiritual immaturity. It's the covering up of those problems that shows spiritual weakness.

Jesus said, "If you are offering your gift at the altar and there remember that your brother has something against you, leave your gift there in front of the altar. First go and be reconciled to your brother; then come and offer your gift" (Matt. 5:23-24).

This passage contains one of the most important relationship principles in the Bible. Jesus says that the moment you realize a relationship problem exists, you should deal with it—even if it means interrupting your religious activities to do so.

The point here is not that our relationships are more important than worship. The point is that devout people *can have* such problems, they interfere with true worship, and they must be dealt with. We can't deal with relationship problems by making offerings to God. We must deal directly with those involved.

When Lorraine and I lived in Alaska and our relationship was rapidly deteriorating, I was very active in the local church and in the Christian community. Lorraine and I were involved in three Bible studies a week. We were leading these studies together, and still we had problems that brought us to the brink of disaster. I was also involved in coordinating a city-wide discipleship training program for a whole group of churches. Yet, in the midst of all this spiritual activity, my primary relationships at home and at work were falling apart.

I felt I had no one to whom I could go. I convinced myself that if I talked with my pastor I would lose credibility as a spiritual leader in the church and the community. And I wanted to avoid that.

Since Lorraine and I were the leaders for the couples in our Bibles studies, giving them guidance, I felt I certainly couldn't go to those people either.

To others it appeared that Lorraine and I had an excellent relationship. Couples even came to us for marriage counseling.

Now, after many years of seeing other people in the same situation I once was, I believe that the more spiritual leadership roles a person assumes, the greater the temptation to suppress relationship problems. Sometimes I find too that non-Christians can admit their relationship problems to others more easily than Christians.

Another reason the Christian leader is reluctant to admit relationship problems is that he really doesn't want to deal with them. He feels he is above such problems. His spiritual stature should protect him somehow. Consequently, he not only has difficulty admitting the problem to others but also may have difficulty admitting it to himself.

A seminary professor on the East Coast recently asked me if I would be shocked to hear he was leaving his wife. After hearing similar things countless times from other spiritual leaders, I wasn't shocked at all. He then told me I was the first person to whom he felt comfortable telling his problem.

"When you come to the point of admitting a problem," I told him, "only then can you start the process of returning to a cooperative relationship."

It took a long time for this simple truth to become clear to me when Lorraine and I were having our problems. For years I was unwilling to admit to myself or Lorraine the existence of serious problems in our marriage. Until I became willing to do so, I could not begin solving them.

But admitting a problem to ourselves is not enough. Admitting our relationship problems to God is not enough either. "Leave your gift there ... first go and be reconciled to yourbrother." We have to admit the problem to the others in the relationship. This is not easy, but the others in the relationship certainly know we have a relationship problem, and they know they have one too.

They could be hiding the problem, unwilling to admit it, but underneath they know it is there.

At work that day when I was wrestling with my five steps to restore my marriage, I went through mental anguish over the first one: "Admit to myself and others" the situation.

I'd run too much risk to my spiritual reputation by admitting this, I thought.

I tussled with that problem for a long time. But the weight of the biblical principal of meeting Lorraine head on with this and getting outside help eventually convicted me of my need to admit the problem openly.

Admit Your Sinfulness

Before I approached Lorraine about admitting our problem, I mentally went on to step two, to see how I should handle that meeting.

The second step in returning to a cooperative relationship is to admit our self-centeredness, and to recognize that this sin has contributed greatly to the problem in the relationship.

Confessing our selfishness as sin is a primary reality for us as Christians. That's how we became Christians in the first place. We knew we were guilty of going our own way. We repented of that, asked Jesus to forgive us, and He did (see Isa. 53:6; Rom. 3:23; 1 John 1:9). The awesome goodness of Jesus and the wonder of God's grace still brings us to our knees in the face of our guilt.

In our human relationships our view of sin and selfishness gets clouded. We must confess both to God and to the person we've wronged that we are guilty. Unfortunately, we frequently find it harder to ask people to forgive us than to ask God.

It was hard enough for me to admit openly that I had a serious problem with Lorraine, but it was so much harder to take the second step and confess that my self-centeredness was the cause. Every time I considered asking Lorraine's forgiveness, I remembered all of my needs she had failed to meet, resulting in hurt feelings and hostility in me. I felt I could never say that the problem was my fault.

Typically, one of the biggest hurdles in restoring a relationship to cooperation is getting over this fault-finding syndrome that develops from unmet needs. As a relationship deteriorates, we develop more and more unmet needs, and we tend to blame the other person more and more for not meeting them. Blaming ourselves is almost out of the question.

I spent weeks in Alaska struggling with that point and arguing with God that I wasn't the one responsible for the deteriorating relationship. Lorraine, I argued, was clearly the one at fault.

One day, out of desperation, I decided to get it all down in writing. I pulled out a notebook and pen and compiled a long list of Lorraine's faults.

When all Lorraine's faults were recorded, I realized it would not look good to God if I just picked on her. After all, I was not perfect. I decided to admit to God that I did have *one* fault. I wrote that my wife had a lot of talents for which I never gave her credit.

However, at the same time I pointed out all the things that I did for her—buying her clothes and cars, and taking her out to all those Mexican restaurants.

In effect, I was passing judgment on her. I was trying to justify in my mind and with God that she was responsible for the relationship failure, not me. And I was trying to prove to God and myself that Lorraine should be the one to ask forgiveness.

The Bible condemns this kind of thinking.

"Why do you judge your brother? Or why do you look down on your brother?" (Rom. 14:10) Why is it that we try to find fault with what our family, spouses, and associates have done or are doing?

A little later in the same passage, we read, "Let us stop passing judgment on one another" (v. 13). And still later— "Let us therefore make every effort to do what leads to peace and to mutual edification" (v. 19).

Ultimately, we cannot deny our self-centeredness. We know that getting our needs met at the other's expense is what caused a deteriorating relationship.

Remember the cooperation style. Our focus is on meeting the needs of others and de-emphasizing ourselves. That is why the relationship is so good and enjoyable. When everyone in the relationship applies that principle, all needs are met.

In isolation, it is totally the opposite. "I'm going to get my needs met whether you do or not. In fact, I will get my needs met at your expense if I have to." That is selfishness, and God calls selfishness sin. As a result, eventually no one's needs are being met.

In order to begin restoring the relationship, I must admit to God and to those I've wronged, "I blew it. I've been selfish. I've been interested in meeting my own needs and not yours. I am sorry, and I ask you to forgive me."

I was sharing this very point with a group of miners in a management seminar not long ago, and a young miner came to me during one of the breaks.

"Are you sure I've got to ask forgiveness to restore a relationship?" he asked, a pained expression on his face.

"Yes, I'm sure," I said. "It has been my experience that without forgiveness the relationship will eventually end."

"I don't think I can do it," he said, worried and looking at the floor.

He then told me his story. He hated his boss. He even came to the point where he contemplated creating a mining accident in which the boss would be killed.

His dislike began when his boss accused him of stealing tools. "I never stole those tools," he said fiercely.

I challenged him to ask forgiveness anyway—not to tell the boss he had thought of killing him, but to confess his anger and animosity. I must admit that I didn't say this easily. Miners live an extremely physical and survival-oriented life. Who knew what might happen if he did this? But the man needed to confess his guilt to his boss. A biblical principle was involved.

I saw him several weeks later.

"Hey, Myron, guess what. It worked!"

He had gone to his boss and told him he was sorry for what he had done deliberately to cause problems in his life. He had said he wanted to patch up their relationship.

His boss was taken aback, and the two ended up having a long talk. The boss apologized too. (If you had ever met the boss, you would know that was a miracle.) Today, those two men are good friends.

The Bible says, "As God's chosen people, holy and dearly loved, clothe yourselves with compassion, kindness, humility, gentleness, and patience. Bear with each other and forgive whatever grievances you may have against one another. Forgive as the Lord forgave you" (Col. 3:12-13).

When I was struggling with the second step to restoring my relationship with Lorraine, it was this Scripture that finally gave me the courage to approach her. Actually, however I still had a wrong spirit. I still assumed that Lorraine was the one with all the faults. After all, I had the list to compare her against me, didn't I? She certainly needed to be forgiven for the way she had treated me, I thought, and I needed to be forgiven for my *one* fault too.

I came home from work and said, "Lorraine, I want to talk with you. Let's go for a ride."

As with many relationships caught in the ice of isolation, ours was dragging on. Though we were at the end of our relationship, we were still living together, each focusing on his or her own personal needs.

We drove to a parking lot overlooking an Alaskan bay. As we sat there, I said, "Lorraine, I want you to know I'm sorry our marriage didn't work out. And it probably was partly my fault that it didn't work."

Notice that I was only saying, "I'm sorry." I wasn't saying, "I'm willing to change."

I then told her I was sorry I hadn't given her proper recognition for her skills, hadn't recognized her talents and abilities.

"I want you to forgive me," I said.

Lorraine was staring straight ahead, out through the window, and wouldn't even look at me. After a long silence, she turned toward me and only responded, "Huh!" as if she despised my apology.

I was immediately incensed. Didn't she recognize that I was crawling on my knees to ask forgiveness when *she* actually should be the one asking, not me? I took the keys out of the car, and I left her sitting there. I walked all the way home with the car keys in my pocket. She had to walk home by herself.

What I had done was give my second point a sort of lip service. I hadn't changed in terms of my commitment to the relationship. I hadn't asked forgiveness, intending to change my ways and to restore the relationship. I was only technically asking for forgiveness.

Commit to Meet the Other's Needs

The third step in getting back to cooperation is to put the other person's needs ahead of your own. It is not enough to admit you are wrong or say, "I'm sorry." You must demonstrate it through your actions. You must put the needs of others first.

Unless you are willing to do that, the relationship can never be restored. Actions speak louder than words.

If we are truly sorry for our past mistakes and the damage they've done to the relationship, we will stop committing those mistakes.

In my personal experience, I found that each step in restoring a relationship was harder than the previous one, not easier. I believe that is why so many people are unwilling to go through the painful process of restoring a relationship. It is one of the most difficult things you can do as a human being.

Putting others' needs before our own shouldn't be so hard to do, but once we are strongly committed emotionally to our own needs, we can't just switch. We feel a self-righteous justification that says, "You've wronged me. I'm only asking now for what is due me."

Up to this point in returning the relationship to cooperation, we have admitted a problem and have admitted our fault. This much does not have to be an entirely humbling experience. We can do this completely for vain reasons.

Many people get this far, but when they have to start meeting the other person's needs they can't make the jump. "I'm sorry, but I can't change. That's just the way I am."

Movies, books, magazines, and other elements reflecting the throw-away and me-centered mentality typical of our generation support this self-centered thinking. However, you can't find it supported anywhere in the Bible.

In my case, I knew the relationship needed to be restored, and I decided to commit to it. But after thinking about myself so long, I had to put it into a context that my emotions could handle.

"Lorraine," I said to myself, "I'm not going to leave you. If anybody leaves, it'll have to be you."

It was self-justification and hurt and determination all mixed together, but it worked.

I should point out here, even though I was very imperfectly applying my five steps for restoring a relationship, they were working. Had I applied them better, they would have worked better. But even my imperfect efforts in the right direction offered hope and help to the relationship.

When I made the decision to put Lorraine's needs first, I was shocked to discover that I no longer even knew what they were. It took me several minutes to figure out one simple need I should meet. I was extremely embarrassed at how selfish I must have been to be so unthinking and inconsiderate.

That's almost always the case of people stuck for some time in an isolation relationship. You simply don't know what your partner's feelings are anymore, where he or she hurts or what he or she cares about.

Each day, I had to work consciously at re-establishing a broken habit of meeting Lorraine's needs. This is what's needed to break out of an isolation relationship style. Even if we are committed to another for the wrong reasons emotionally, we will begin to see some changes.

Since we're not emotionally in tune with the other person, it will be *work* to meet the person's needs. We will probably resent it. We may even be mechanical in doing it. But we are building a habit, working backward, if you will.

We no longer have the advantage of early relationship excitement to propel us. But we have another motivating factor. The awful atmosphere of our isolation relationship will begin to change. We will be carried along by a return to the relationship that originally motivated us to meet the needs of our partner.

Patient and Kind

Once we get committed to restoring a relationship, for whatever emotional reasons, we have to work at meeting the other person's needs.

The fourth thing I wrote down on my list in the park that day was, "Act out 1 Corinthians 13:4-8." It is one of the most popular passages in the Bible describing love in action. "Love is patient, love is kind. It does not envy, it does not boast, it is not proud. It is not rude, it is not self-seeking, it is not easily angered, it keeps no record of wrongs. Love does not delight in evil but rejoices with the truth. It always protects, always trusts, always hopes, always perseveres."

In isolation, we are acting out of selfishness. We have forgotten completely what a love action is. That is why this fourth step is so critical.

We now have to do what love does. At first, it is something that we "act" out. We perform deeds of love, though we don't feel like it. Our emotions don't want to love, so we have to force ourselves to take the actions that demonstrate love. This is very painful, but look at the alternative. We can "be ourselves," as some modern psychologists might advise, and act out our hateful emotions. Or we can consciously act out love, refusing to submit to our selfish emotions. It's not that we hide our selfishness or hurt. No, we are refusing to act out the consequences of it, choosing to act out love instead.

I knew this is what I had to do with Lorraine, though I didn't feel like doing it. Lorraine was not convinced of any change in my ways, because she hadn't seen any. I had asked her for forgiveness, but hadn't made a commitment to meet her needs in the relationship.

However, even making that commitment was not going to

return us to cooperation. I needed to do something more. I desperately needed to love Lorraine. That is, I needed to put 1 Corinthians 13:4-8 into visible action.

After all those years of marriage, I found myself in a strange position. I had to give myself "assignments" each day—things to do to demonstrate kindness, patience, and all the biblical expressions of love. I wasn't used to loving anymore, and I needed to practice.

"I like the way your hair looks."

"I really enjoyed the meal tonight, Lorraine."

It was very robotlike, but it was an outward change. Such statements were going against my emotions. I was thinking that she should be the one saying nice things to me, but I forced myself to think of her and her needs first.

It was an extremely difficult process to go through. But over a period of weeks, after consistently giving myself assignments to demonstrate love and then following through, something began happening to me.

I came home from work one day, started up the stairs, and then stopped to look in the kitchen. I saw that Lorraine had a new hairdo.

Without thinking about it, I said, "Hey, Lorraine, I really think your hair looks nice."

It dawned on me right then that I hadn't written down that statement as an assignment for the day. That may seem like a natural thing to have said, but when you're in isolation, that kind of compliment is out of the question.

I was coming out of isolation! I was changing! Over a period of time, I continued to faithfully apply the love principles of 1 Corinthians and, as a result, my feelings of love continued to grow. It was a long process, but each step forward was exciting.

I believe this fourth step is the hardest of all the steps back to cooperation. But there is absolutely no way back to cooperation without it. You can't short-cut the process. I began learning that *feelings* of love follow *actions* of love.

Thank God

The last step in the process of returning to cooperation is to begin thanking God for the individual in the relationship and his or her positive contribution to it. We must admit that we really do need the other person in the relationship.

This thankful attitude forces us to focus on the positive traits of an individual. Instead of practicing the mental habit of disgust at a person's faults, we praise his or her qualities.

Philippians 4:8 tells us, "Finally, brothers, whatever is true, whatever is noble, whatever is right, whatever is pure, whatever is lovely, whatever is admirable—if anything is excellent or praiseworthy—think about such things." This verse establishes the ground rules for living cooperatively with our partners. It challenges us to always focus on positive thoughts.

Remember, a relationship will deteriorate when we think negatively of a person and positively of ourselves instead. Thoughts of criticism, condemning, and complaining drag down our partner in our eyes and elevate us. But we can't act this way if we are focusing on the positive qualities of a person and thanking God for the person.

How Far Must We Deteriorate?

During relationship seminars, people frequently ask me if it's necessary for a relationship to deteriorate completely to isolation before applying these five steps back to a cooperative style relationship. The obvious answer is no. If we wait to apply these steps until we get to isolation, we are putting the relationship in jeopardy. The path back may be too difficult. The longer you wait, the more difficult your changes are. As soon as you identify a problem in the relationship, immediately apply this process.

Never forget that relationships *always* have problems. But, instead of moving silently and expectantly into retaliation, crashing into domination, and screeching a relationship to a final halt in isolation, admit the problem right away. And begin demonstrating love whether you feel like it or not.

Will people think you are just mechanically acting out

"love" for them? They might. But the proof is going to be your commitment to continue the process, and your desire to act out love in order to restore the relationship to full, true love. True love always focuses on meeting the needs of the other person.

At first, your partner will probably recognize that something is odd in your behavior. He or she may complain that you are just putting on. And that may be partly true. You may be demonstrating acts of love without feelings of love. But if you are committed to continuing, over a period of time the feelings will follow the actions. Unfortunately, most of us won't allow the time needed to reestablish the feelings of love that come from performing acts of love. However, I can tell you from my own experience that the results are worth all the effort.

8

Handling Conflict

You likely have no trouble agreeing with Proverbs 17:1, which says, "Better is a dry crust with peace and quiet than a house full of feasting, with strife."

All of us would agree that conflict is unpleasant, and something to be avoided when possible.

Nevertheless, conflict occurs in all relationships arising whenever we have direct disagreements with others and end up openly opposed to them.

Because we all need for others to accept our ideas and feelings, conflict is going to be inevitable in our relationships. People don't have identical ideas and feelings, and our need for acceptance of our ideas and feelings sets us up for open opposition.

We know from previous chapters that if our ideas and feelings get rejected, we end up with unmet needs.

Two things tend to happen when unmet needs create conflict:

1. We try to impose our ideas and feelings on others.

2. We resist others' attempts to impose their ideas and feelings on us.

Throughout this chapter, we will be saying the following in a number of different ways. *In resolving conflict, we must look at the situation from the other's perspective, knowing that resisting others and imposing our ideas on them can only increase conflict.*

God's dealing with Moses as recorded in Exodus 3:7—4:17 gives us the classic example of how we should take another person's perspective. First, God's thoughts and feelings about His people take into account their perspectives. Second, God resolves conflict with Moses by looking at matters from his perspective.

In no less than a dozen instances in this passage, God sees that Moses isn't agreeing with Him. Each time, God accommodates Moses' viewpoint and helps him overcome his concerns, his worry, and his outright knee-shaking fear about going back to Egypt to lead the people out of bondage.

One of the reasons a person in isolation develops a feeling of hopelessness and despair is that conflicts increase. In this chapter, we want to examine various faulty ways people try to solve conflict. We will also consider biblical principles for dealing with conflict properly.

We Don't Know How to Deal with Conflict

A major problem of society is people's lack of know-how in dealing with conflict. We have been programmed from childhood to view conflict as something bad that we should avoid at almost any cost.

Most adults don't know how to deal with conflict, so they can't teach their children to handle it either. Parents frequently scold children, telling them to "stop fighting" when an argument develops between them.

Recently I was in the home of friends who have two children. Both wanted the same toy, and soon they were pulling at it and yelling at each other. The father got out of his chair, took the toy from them, and sent them to their rooms. "Stay there until you can get along with each other," he said.

Chances are that those two children are never going to learn to "get along with each other," because they end up in separate rooms.

No relationship can exist for long without conflict. Therefore, learning to deal with conflict actually means dealing with relationships.

I raised my children the same way my friends did whom I just cited. Most parents do. The same approach carries onto the school playgrounds too. It's because society doesn't understand how to handle conflict, and therefore chooses to avoid it.

Most of us adults operate on the premise that conflict leads to a no-win situation.

When Lorraine and I were at odds in Alaska, we ended up in perpetual conflict by the time we reached isolation. Avoiding conflict any further was simply impossible. Our only recourse was either to deal finally with the conflict, or to see the relationship end.

Lack of training in dealing effectively with conflict is one of the major reasons people wind up in isolation relationships.

During my relationships seminars, people frequently tell me that they feel helpless when a conflict develops. They don't know how to deal with it.

They run into conflict situations that don't get solved, so they keep repeating their mistakes. As conflicts increase, so does the frustration. Eventually people conclude the situation is hopeless simply because they don't know how to deal with conflict.

I had coffee recently with Don Baker, the owner and operator of a large construction firm. Don told me he was a member of his church board and was in conflict with his pastor over the size and type of new church building they were constructing for the community.

"I'd rather take a beating on this entire project than go through the torture of sitting through another meeting with that man," he said.

Apparently, any meeting he had with the pastor ended in an argument. "I get uptight just thinking about it," he said. "He's insisting on getting a million-dollar building for half that price, and I'm at the end of my rope." Many of us end up in situations similar to Don's. We want nothing more than to solve our conflict problems. We aren't seeking revenge. We don't even have to see ourselves win. We'd just like to end the conflict, but we don't have the training necessary to do so.

Different Perspectives Breed Resistance

In the Exodus passage cited earlier, we really see a difference between God's perspective and Moses'. God tells Moses, "I have indeed seen the misery of My people in Egypt. I have heard them crying out because of their slave drivers, and I am concerned about their suffering" (Ex. 3:7).

God's perspective centered on the needs of His people. He proposed that Moses go down to Egypt and deliver His people from Pharaoh.

Moses responded, "Who am I, that I should go to Pharaoh and bring the Israelites out of Egypt?" (v. 11)

Moses' perspective centered on his memory of being in Egypt, where Pharaoh had once kicked him out. He was afraid for his skin, and was operating from a self-preserving perspective.

Through the rest of the chapter, Moses continues with his self-preserving thinking. He keeps getting into conflict with God—giving excuses about not being able to speak well, saying Pharaoh would not believe a stupid-looking shepherd, and so on.

God accommodated Moses' perspective all the time, and simply answered each of Moses' fears with a solution. Running up against resistance from Moses didn't shock God, and such reactions shouldn't shock us.

"A man who lacks judgment derides his neighbor" (Prov. 11:12). Now, God certainly doesn't lack judgment and He wasn't about to deride Moses. Hammering away at Moses by putting down his ideas and feelings wasn't God's way. He didn't bend Moses' will either. He just kept responding to Moses' fears until His servant decided to take a shot at seeing God's perspective in the situation.

We could all learn something from God's dealing with Moses. Most of us tend to attack and belittle others when their perspective is different from ours. This never solves conflict. It only intensifies it. The first step calls for looking at the situation from the other person's point of view, rather than simply trying to impose our own will on others.

Conflict Is an Opportunity

If everyone's ideas and feelings in a relationship were the same, we would be in harmony. Since they are different, the promotion of our own ideas and feelings is really a way of stating our needs.

When we are in conflict and openly opposing each other, we are not listening to each other. We are simply promoting our own needs and perspective, and overlooking those of others.

I do a lot of traveling and eat too much in restaurants. I get sick of it. When I got off the airplane after a long series of restaurant meals recently, I had it fixed in my mind that I would go right home and have a home-cooked meal.

Lorraine, on the other hand, was waiting for me at the airport all dressed to go out to dinner. She was sick of staying at home and fixing her own meals. She wanted to eat at a fancy restaurant when I arrived.

We were both smiling, and greeted each other warmly when I got off the plane. Lorraine hugged me and said, "Myron, where do you want to go to eat?"

This was a perfect opportunity for me to meet a need she had. She was obviously dressed to go out, and she was sincerely giving me a choice of any place I wanted to go, including a Mexican restaurant.

Had I been sensitive to Lorraine's need, I would have recognized the opportunity to meet it. But all I was thinking about was my own need, which ran counter to hers.

"You know what I'd like, Lorraine?" I said. "I'd like to go home and just have a peanut butter sandwich or something simple like that."

By the time we had walked from the airport to the car,

Lorraine was getting upset with me, because she had gone to a great deal of work to get dressed to go out on the town.

When we realize that we are approaching a conflict, we have to ask ourselves what the other person's needs are. We must always keep in mind that opposing needs are at the heart of every relationship conflict. If we are committed to meeting the other person's needs, then conflict provides an excellent reminder of what they are.

Before we drove away from the airport, I finally realized that Lorraine had a big need. She was tired of eating at home and needed an evening out. I suggested that we go to her favorite Chinese restaurant, and we had a great evening together.

Had I insisted on focusing on my own need at her expense, we might have spent a miserable evening at home.

In the midst of promoting our own self interest, it is difficult to see another's needs because our emotions get in the way. But when another person's feelings are being expressed, we should look for the opportunity to meet his or her needs instead of our own.

However, this does not mean that the only way to solve a conflict is always to give in and let the other person have his way. Always giving in sets the stage for domination and eventually an isolation relationship.

When my attitude is, "I'll give in to you this time," I really am looking at my own needs and not yours. And I'm probably feeling self-righteous for playing the martyr.

On the other hand, in a true cooperation relationship each person has a sincere desire to meet the other person's needs. Each honestly desires to think of the other first.

Forgive in Place of Judging

Forgiveness is the best way to ward off retaliation. When we judge each other—condemn actions, thoughts, ideas, and feelings—it encourages others in the relationship to enter a retaliation mode to defend and justify themselves.

One of the best ways to deal with conflict and to keep

retaliation from building is to avoid judging the feelings of others.

Even if another person's idea, feeling, thought, or action needs correction, we aren't likely to correct it through criticism.

Jesus showed a better way. On one occasion, the religious leaders brought to Jesus a woman they had caught in the act of adultery. According to the religious law of the day, this woman should have been stoned to death. When they asked Jesus His view on this, He said, "If any one of you is without sin, let him be the first to throw a stone at her" (John 8:7, NIV).

After everyone had gone, leaving their stones on the ground, Jesus said, "Woman, where are they? Has no one condemned you?" (v. 10)

Jesus had every right to condemn her. He would have been perfectly justified in whipping out the Ten Commandments, rattling off number seven, and dropping His thumb as a signal to let the stones fly.

Instead, He corrected her by forgiving her. Forgiveness restores relationships. Judgment destroys them.

Unless we are willing to completely ignore and forget the past mistakes of others, we will never get back to cooperative relationships. By remembering others' errors, and wielding them as clubs, we judge our relationships into oblivion.

Conflicts Are Not Bad

The starting point in dealing with conflict successfully is to realize that conflicts are not necessarily bad. They can be the opposite—a source of improving a relationship.

We have two options in dealing with conflict:

1. We can conclude conflict is bad and should be avoided at all costs.

2. We can conclude conflict is a normal feature of relationships, and provides an opportunity to better understand one another and bring about mutual benefit when used to identify and meet each other's needs.

If you think conflict should be avoided at all costs, you'll become defensive when approaching a conflict situation. You will maintain a guarded role.

You will also be unwilling to be totally honest about how you feel, especially if you believe it will lead to conflict.

Lorraine and I used to do this all the time. In the early stages of repairing our relationship when everything was so fragile, we were even more cautious.

When our relationship was degenerating, both of us viewed conflict as something we should avoid. We suppressed our real feelings and thoughts on certain issues in an effort to avoid arguments.

Unfortunately, this didn't change the way we thought or felt. Those feelings were still there festering. They eventually surfaced in a highly emotional atmosphere.

The most tragic ramification of concluding that conflict is bad is the suppression of the real self. It blocks open communication, and we end up communicating only on safe issues.

On the other hand, if we conclude that conflicts are a normal feature of relationships we are not greatly threatened by opposing viewpoints. We are willing to communicate what we really think and how we really feel.

One of the key ingredients to maintaining a cooperative relationship is the attitude that conflict is healthy and not something to be avoided.

Conflict creates an opportunity for us to know each other better and to serve each other more.

When Abraham and Lot were caught in a conflict over the land, Abraham didn't try to avoid conflict (Gen. 13). He approached the problem head on, seeing this as an opportunity to serve his nephew by putting the younger man's needs ahead of his own.

Options Other than Conflict

We have four options when approaching a conflict situation. Our first is to see the conflict, recognize it as one, and then retreat (as shown in figure 8).

Figure 8. When we realize we are approaching a conflict, many of us tend to retreat, thinking it will go away. Conflicts are never resolved using this approach.

This is the standard form we are taught in our society. It is a way of fulfilling the goal of self-preservation.

I have a dear friend who was pastor of a church. He went to college four years, majoring in Bible. Then he went on for three more years to seminary. Finally he became pastor of a large church in the midwest.

He had a lovely wife, seen by most people as the ideal pastor's wife. She could play the piano, lead the singing, head up vaious ladies groups, and do all of the other things usually expected of a pastor's wife.

Many people said that someday my friend would be one of the major leaders of his denomination. But underneath all of their successful appearance, this pastor and his wife had serious problems in their relationship, particularly money.

A pastor isn't usually the highest paid citizen in the community, and these two often suffered financial hardships. His viewpoint was that poverty came with the job. He nurtured something of a martyr complex and almost welcomed being poorer than he really needed to be. By contrast, she had come from an affluent family and had difficulty adjusting to being denied what she needed or even what she wanted.

Both realized they had great differences of opinion in regard to dealing with finances, but they felt the way to maintain a proper relationship in the church community was to avoid the issue. They didn't believe that heated arguments were good signs of a healthy pastor/wife relationship. In fact, they viewed any such exchange as spiritual weakness.

Whenever the subject of money or their finances came up in discussion, they would duck the issue. She wanted to drive a nice new car, but he thought that was not the proper image for a pastor and his wife. She also wanted nice clothes, but they didn't discuss that beyond her initial request either.

Ten years into the marriage, while pastoring one of the largest churches in the city, my friend got out of bed one morning and found a note from his wife on her pillow beside him.

She said she could no longer subject herself to his value system. She could not continue portraying the suffering couple for the Gospel, remaining in poverty so people wouldn't suspect that they might love money.

She left him and eventually they were divorced.

They both knew there was a conflict all through their years together. He was educated and she was capable in her role as pastor's wife. Yet, every time the issue arose, they retreated from it, as if it would just go away.

But issues don't go away. They stay there, waiting and getting bigger as we postpone dealing with them.

Trying to ignore and retreat from conflict is not a satisfactory method of dealing with a growing issue.

Ephesians 4:26 says, "In your anger do not sin: Do not let the sun go down while you are still angry." This means when we disagree and our opposing views lead to conflict, we should deal with it immediately. We shouldn't ignore it and retreat from it, but admit it and resolve it.

In fact, the verse is saying that as a conflict develops it should be dealt with and resolved before the end of the day.

Figure 9. Another way we attempt to deal with conflict is to skirt the issues involved. However, this approach only increases the size of the conflict and makes it increasingly difficult to solve.

My friend and his wife violated that principle, and it eventually destroyed their relationship.

Talk Our Way Around the Issue

A second way people deal with conflicts is similar to the first. We identify a conflict issue, but we try to talk our way all around it, as illustrated in figure 9.

Talk does not resolve conflict unless it focuses on the real issues of the problem. Ignoring this seemingly obvious principle, many people try to make an "end run" around the issues by increasing the speed and flow of the conversation.

This approach lets the unresolved problems remain, even if you did manage to talk your way around them for the moment. The problems will surface later, bigger than ever.

While working as a personnel director in private industry, I learned the folly of trying to skirt conflict. A secretary from another division wanted to transfer to our department, but every time she brought up the subject she had problems with me. I felt she lacked the skills and experience required for the job, but I didn't want to hurt her feelings. So every time she asked why I wouldn't let her transfer, I changed the subject.

One day, shortly after I promoted a male employee, I received a call from the local civil rights office; the secretary I was ignoring had registered a complaint.

She accused me of sex discrimination because I would not let her advance her career. She charged I was holding her back simply because she was a woman. My attempts to avoid the issue had only made the problem worse.

As a management consultant, I've seen this approach as the most prevalent way of dealing with conflict in business. For instance, managers who know their employees are upset with the way things are handled try to justify their position without really dealing with the true issue in contention.

In union and management situations, employers and employees rarely deal directly with the issues that concern either side, unless they are forced to. There is little sincerity or honest dealing with their relationship. But unless we are honest with one another, we can't build a trust relationship and live or work in cooperation.

Trying to talk our way around conflict only increases the level of mistrust and confusion that frequently accompanies conflict situations.

Dealing with Side Issues

A third way we deal with conflicts is the most destructive of all. We avoid confronting the issue and deal with a side issue, trying to communicate in an indirect fashion (see figure 10).

Our purpose in dealing with side issues is to communicate how we feel about the conflict situation. But it doesn't work.

Several years ago, Lorraine worked as executive secretary for a university president. Four secretaries worked in the office plus an office manager.

One of the secretaries had a serious body odor problem, which became a major conversation point among the rest of the secretaries. For weeks they tried to get the office manager to go to the secretary and confront her with the problem.

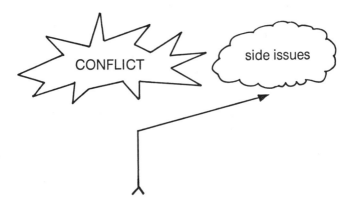

Figure 10. Some of us try to solve conflict by focusing on various side issues. Instead of solving the conflict this approach usually develops new conflict areas within the relationship.

This prospect was embarrassing for the office manager, so she decided to avoid doing anything.

The longer the problem went on, the more embarrassing it became for the girls in the office. They got more and more upset with the manager.

Finally, the office manager tried to solve the problem. At the end of the day, the secretaries were all leaving the office. The girl with the offensive odor was walking out the door right in front of the office manager. In a voice everyone could hear, the manager said to another secretary, "Have you ever tried deodorant? It really works well!"

The girl she was shouting at didn't understand what she was doing, and was extremely insulted that the manager implied that she had body odor. The whole thing erupted into a confused exchange, the girl with the problem never was confronted, and she continued to have body odor.

Many of us use tactics like this over and over. I used to do it with Lorraine, trying to communicate a thought or feeling to her by talking about a side issue. It always ended up creating a separate problem rather than resolving the original conflict.

Facing Conflict Head On

The only way to deal with conflict successfully is to identify it and face it head on (see figure 11). Sidestepping, avoiding, and talking about something completely different only causes more problems, and increases the intensity of the conflict.

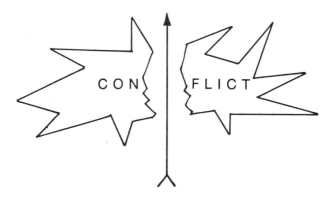

Figure 11. The proper way to deal with conflict is to approach it head on, identifying the real issues involved and working our way through them. This is the only way to actually resolve the problem. However, since it can be a frustrating and unpleasant experience, most of us tend to avoid this method as long as possible.

When we face conflict head on, there are five rules that should be followed.

First: *Always attack the problem, never the person.* Abraham and Lot faced a conflict because there wasn't enough water for their herds. This was creating tension.

Abraham could have attacked Lot verbally, using his dignity of age, his position, and his calling from God. "Lot, you are being a very selfish person when you really have no right to the water." But Abraham didn't.

Abraham focused on the problem, and purposely avoided attacking Lot as a person. He knew Lot really wasn't right in his intentions, and he also knew he would be justified in telling Lot to pack up the sandals he started with and trek off on his own. But Abraham also knew that the problem was one of water, and that Lot's personality was secondary.

Abraham stuck to the real issue, making sure he didn't wind up condemning or faulting the person in the process.

When we see a person as the problem, we force him to go on the defensive and he will probably counterattack. He can always find fault with us, and the conflict turns into an argument over who's to blame. This never solves conflict.

I was recently involved with three other people in a business arrangement. Each of us had a different view of a problem. We couldn't see eye to eye on the cause of it, and the problem began affecting the business arrangement itself.

We held a meeting to resolve it. During the first few minutes, one of the partners pointed his finger in the face of another fellow and accused him of starting the problem.

The partner being attacked countered by justifying his position, and saying that his accuser was the cause of the problem. They went back and forth like this while I sat there trying to make heads or tails of the whole thing. After fifteen minutes, we had to end the meeting and nothing was accomplished. We still were unresolved at the writing of this book.

"A man who lacks judgment derides his neighbor, but a man of understanding holds his tongue" (Prov. 11:12). Don't deride or attack the other person.

The second rule to follow is: *Always verbalize feelings, and never act them out.*

When someone does something that upsets you, tell him it upsets you. Don't sulk, or pout, or give him the silent treatment to communicate your disapproval.

This was one of the hardest rules for Lorraine and me to learn on our road back to cooperation. We used to communicate our disapproval by our actions.

For example, Lorraine used to clam up and refuse to talk about a problem. After hours of silence, I would get the picture that something was wrong and finally I would ask what it was. She would simply say, "Nothing."

This would start a guessing game of "twenty questions" as I tried to figure out what I had done to upset her.

The action approach does communicate your disapproval about something, but it doesn't get at what is wrong.

The third rule for dealing with conflict is: *Be willing to forgive instead of judging the other person.* It is easy for us to justify our own actions and condemn those of other people. But justifying yourself and condemning others never resolves conflict.

Jesus said, "Why do you look at the speck of sawdust in your brother's eye and pay no attention to the plank in your own eye?" (Matt. 7:3)

We have just as many problems and faults as the other people in our relationships. It is useless in a conflict to identify which person is at fault. Yet it's one of the first things we bring up in dealing with a conflict.

If you try to put yourself in the place of Jesus during the events that led up to His crucifixion, it's unbelievable to see the way He maintained a nonjudgmental attitude. He was spat on, beat, mocked, tortured, and mercilessly killed. Yet, as He was dying, He asked God to forgive His killers. It seems pretty clear that they were wrong, but He did nothing to them. He said they didn't know what they were doing.

Jesus demonstrated the attitude that we should have in far less serious circumstances. Instead of accusing and retaliating, we should forgive.

We never resolve conflict through retaliation. We only add to the problem.

The fourth rule is: *Be willing to give more than you take.* Everyone wants to win in a conflict, but that motivation creates more conflict, not resolution. Jesus expressed a key principle concerning giving when He said, "Give, and it will be given to you. A good measure, pressed down, shaken together and running over, will be poured into your lap" (Luke 6:38). In other words, we get back more than we give. This is one of the most important relationship principles we can learn.

By contrast, Lot approached conflict over water rights from

a selfish perspective. He had no concern for Abraham and his needs. He saw the solution to the problem only in his own terms. He wanted the fertile valley—all of it. And he didn't want to give anything in return.

Abraham was willing to give. He wanted resolution, and gave more than he took.

Most of us go into conflict with the attitude that we've got to win this struggle. We want to emerge with our ideas and opinions intact. As long as we are committed to that, conflict escalates.

What we should do is go into a conflict wanting to know the view and opinions of the other. Then we can give as it is appropriate and meet the other's needs. In the giving, our own needs will be met.

Even though Lot's selfishness allowed him to get the best land initially, God saw to it that Abraham's giving spirit made him the winner.

After Lot selfishly took the fertile green valley and left Abraham the rocky desert, God said to Abraham, "Lift up your eyes from where you are and look north and south, east and west. All the land that you see I will give to you and your offspring forever" (Gen. 13:14-15).

Being willing to give really didn't cost Abraham anything in the long run. He could meet Lot's need in the conflict, knowing God would meet his needs.

The last rule for handling conflict is: *Don't just talk, develop understanding.*

When we go into a conflict, we usually are highly emotional and don't have control over our tongues. As a result, we say things we should not.

Proverbs 10:19 says, "When words are many, sin is not absent."

The trap we fall into when conflict arises is allowing our emotions to take over. We don't develop understanding about the issue or how to resolve it. We simply release our emotional tension.

Unless we arrive at understanding, we will completely miss

the goal of meeting another person's needs. Since conflicts arise around unmet needs, they provide us an excellent opportunity to meet another's needs. However, these needs can only be met when we understand what they are.

9

Turning an Ordinary Relationship into an Exciting, Productive Team

Jesus once told the Pharisees, "If a kingdom is divided against itself, that kingdom cannot stand. If a house is divided against itself, that house cannot stand" (Mark 3:24-25).

Jesus used both the large group (kingdom) and the small group (household) to explain that no matter how many or few people are involved in a relationship, if there is division and lack of teamwork, the group will not survive for long.

Teamwork is being unified in effort. It is the mortar that holds a relationship together. Teamwork is one of the most powerful phenomena in group dynamics.

We've all heard of athletic teams lacking skills, experience, and finesse that nevertheless went on to accomplish great things because the group was united and committed in teamwork.

The opposite is also true. Lack of teamwork can cause the most talented group to be unproductive. Business partnerships and marriages that seem to have everything going for them fail. They fail simply because the people did not learn to work together.

Richard and Margaret Blake owned a real estate business. Both had Ivy League educations, and both came from well-to-do families. They were attractive and ambitious.

Neighbors thought of Rich and Margaret as the epitome of American success. For a few years, they were. They were successful in their business, their marriage, and everything they pursued.

The key was their ability to work well together. They complemented each other in talents, and developed an extremely successful real estate business. Rich could bring prospective buyers and sellers together, and Margaret could make them want to close the deal. They seemed unstoppable. When they were negotiating, you just knew they would conclude a real estate contract that would satisfy all the parties.

On top of their business success, they were community leaders. Rich was a member of city council. Margaret taught part-time real estate courses at the university.

At the peak of their combined careers Rich and Margaret let go of the one thing that had made them successful together— teamwork.

One day Margaret called my wife in tears, explaining that Rich had just moved out. Lorraine was taken completely by surprise.

Over the next few weeks, Lorraine began spending a lot of time with Margaret. She discovered that for the last several months, instead of working as a team, Rich and Margaret had been competing against each other.

It was a simple game of competition at first; then it got more serious. The more they competed, the less they kept sight of their common goal of a prosperous relationship.

Eventually, Rich became jealous of his wife's success. She was completing real estate deals he wanted to put together himself.

He was also being embarrassed at various real estate meetings in the community because peers would ask him when Margaret was going to fire him. So he began demanding that she spend more time in the home.

Over a short period of time, what had seemed to be a firmly cemented and lasting relationship ended up in divorce and lawsuits over land holdings.

But the tragedy didn't end there. Their experience of team work gone sour practically destroyed the imagination and trust they needed to work with others in anything.

The last Lorraine and I heard, the two were totally miserable. Rich was working in some dinky town in the Southwest as a carpenter. Hurt and dejected, he had let all his talents in real estate go to waste completely. Margaret wasn't faring much better.

It all happened when sin crept in and Margaret and Rich stopped operating as a team. As quoted earlier, "A house divided against itself cannot stand." Here, the Bible clearly points out the important role teamwork plays in maintaining cooperative relationships. Rich and Margaret demonstrated the validity of Jesus' words.

Developing and Maintaining Teamwork

In this chapter we want to explore what holds a relationship together and keeps it focused in a direction of cooperation.

In earlier chapters, we pointed out that all relationships start in a cooperation style. Therefore, it's very easy for teamwork to develop. However, it is usually difficult to keep it going.

We've said it before, but we need to keep saying it: *The goal in relationships ultimately must be to meet the needs of all those in the relationship.* The framework and the process of meeting needs will vary from person to person and from need to need, but the goal will never change. We must meet the needs of everyone in the relationship.

Initially in relationships, we have all the ingredients of a working team to make the dynamics positive. These ingredients can be found in the simple definition: *A team is two or more people moving along a path of interaction toward a common goal.*

According to the definition, there are three key features of an effective team:

1. A team contains two or more people.
2. There is effective interaction and communication.

3. There is a common goal.

If any one of these three features is missing, we don't really have a team.

The Superperson Myth

An underlying basis of relationships is the recognition that all of us have strengths and weaknesses. I have strengths and weaknesses, and so do you. Unless we recognize that, we will never be effective as team players.

The bottom line, then, is: *Always operate from a mode of strengths, not weaknesses.* My strengths help meet your needs, and your strengths meet mine. We read in Ecclesiastes, "Two are better than one, because they have a good return for their work: if one falls down, his friend can help him up. But pity on the man who falls and has no one to help him up!" (4:9-10)

Figure 12 shows an ideal or complete individual. He is a person of all strengths and no weaknesses. In reality this person does not exist. He is only an idealized concept of the

Figure 12. Even though some of us hate to admit it, none of us are perfect. We all have weaknesses. In a productive team effort we allow others to use their strengths to compensate for our weaknesses.

mind. However, it's difficult to convince some people they are not close to all-knowing and all-powerful.

When I played on a college basketball team, I knew, as did the other players, what our respective strengths were on the court. Each of us looked for teammates to be open to take shots or make rebounds. It was obvious that no one of us had the ability single-handedly to defeat another team.

In contrast to the superperson of figure 12, the real individual is comprised of both strengths and weaknesses (see figure 13). This is the way God made us. We need to form relationships with others to compensate for our weaknesses.

When I do relationship-building seminars, I begin by assigning people to write a list of their own individual strengths and weaknesses as they perceive them. Next, they are asked to write weaknesses and strengths of their team. Then they share the results with their team members at the seminar.

It's fascinating to watch the mental gyrations that result. People seem to run into two problems:

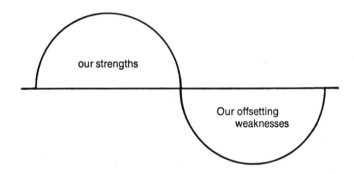

Figure 13. In order for a team to have meaningful relationships, its members must realize that each person has strengths and weaknesses. If we spend all of our time focusing on our weaknesses, they tend to offset our strengths.

1. It is hard to be introspective about strengths and weaknesses and accurate at the same time. However, it's important to try to analyze the traits. We cannot operate as a team member and develop a team mentality without in some degree knowing our strengths and weaknesses.

2. It is difficult to communicate our personal weaknesses to the team. However, that's important too. We must communicate our individual strengths and weaknesses if we are to grow as a team.

Rich and Margaret put together a profitable real estate and land development business when they operated on the basis of each other's strengths. Rich was fantastic in prospecting for potential buyers. He seemed to have a nose for where the money was. Margaret was terrific at closing a sale. When they combined these strengths, they became a highly successful team.

In order to develop a strong team, then, two things must be clear to everyone in the relationship:

1. The partners must identify areas where each can serve the other.

2. The partners must understand at what points they need each other.

Once we do these two things, we can understand why we need the relationship. The superman in figure 12 isn't aware that he has any needs. That is why he has poor relationships.

In putting together a strong team, we need people who are strong where we are weak (see figure 14). People that have strengths where we have weaknesses will make good relationship partners for us. In turn, where they have weaknesses, we should have strengths. That is the key to effective teamwork.

Consequently, for us to work well together, I should be willing to let your strength serve my weakness, and you should be willing to accept my strength in helping your weakness.

That establishes the criteria for the relationship. We *need* each other.

We've all heard the cliche, "Opposites tend to attract." In

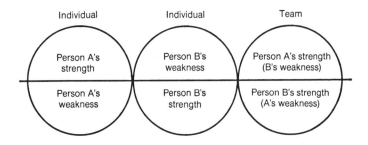

Figure 14. This diagram illustrates how an effective team uses the strengths of one person to compensate for the weaknesses of another. In other words, the effect of our weakness on the relationship is minimized because of the other person's strength.

order to have effective relationships, that's the way it should be. People with the same strengths and weaknesses, can't do much for each other, because they don't need each other.

Identify Strengths and Weaknesses

It's important for people in every business relationship, marriage, and friendship to identify their strengths and weaknesses so they can see how best to serve the needs of their partners.

This process of identifying each other's strengths and weaknesses involves some risk, however. It makes us vulnerable to attack if our intended partner chooses to go that route.

Remember the two couples we introduced in chapter 3? One couple had a need for friendship and the other a need for spiritual nurture. Both knew what they needed and realistically expected the other to provide it. Therefore they found the risk easy to take.

When we move into retaliation, however, the risk of exposing any weaknesss becomes too great. The inclination is to start criticizing and complaining and condemning each other for weaknesses instead of simply identifying them so that the partner can compensate for them.

Often we will begin to believe that we are better than the other person and develop a savior complex, trying to help another person eliminate his areas of weakness.

That is the *worst* thing we can do. I know that sounds atrocious to some, but it is true. It is very important that eliminating the weaknesses in another person never becomes the goal of a relationships.

First of all, it won't happen. People simply don't become all strength. Second it doesn't need to happen. A person can operate from his strengths, despite his weaknesses. Third, it's counterproductive, because focusing on a person's weaknesses undermines his strengths.

In essence, we eliminate the need for any relationship at all by setting as our goal the elimination of another's weakness. It is no longer a cooperative relationship, but a domination relationship.

Eliminating weaknesses is not a bad thing, but it is not a good goal for a relationship.

As figure 15 shows, it is possible and even healthy to have one function of the relationship minimize some of the weaknesses, but we should never focus on that or make it the goal.

Let's say you are my boss, and we identify my strengths and weaknesses. We make a goal of eliminating my weaknesses. Now that sounds like a noble goal, but it will be a disaster to our relationship, and can actually destroy me.

By working with me, we may reduce my weaknesses by 50 percent. However, all of the time, energy, and effort that went into minimizing my weaknesses took away from my areas of strength, as represented by line b of figure 15.

The only contribution I can make in relationships is from my strengths. I serve you with my strengths, not my weaknesses. If the goal of our relationship becomes the elimination of my weaknesses, I make little or no contribution in my areas of strength. I'm certainly not helping you in your needs.

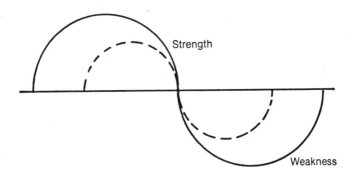

Figure 15. This chart illustrates that it is possible to minimize our personal weaknesses. However, if too much time is spent focusing on our weaknesses (dotted line, b), our strengths greatly suffer. Instead of trying to do away with all of our personal weaknesses, we should be willing to let other people use their strengths where we are weak.

I become a mediocre person, because we've kept me from operating from my strengths. You're going to wind up frustrated, and in conflict with me. We started the relationship on a mode of weakness, and that's all we got out of it—more weakness.

To illustrate the problem, consider a Christian couples seminar that Lorraine and I attended several years ago.

At this seminar, we heard a lot of the popular religious rhetoric describing the ideal modern Christian couple. We were told among other things that it is the man's godly duty to be in charge of the checkbook.

The seminar speaker went even further. He said that if the man isn't the one who carries the checkbook in his pocket and writes all the checks, then the couple is probably living in sin. "That's the man's job," he said emphatically. "How can you be in charge of your home without being in charge of your finances?" he asked, putting a lid on the discussion.

Lorraine and I looked at each other and decided we'd better stop living in sin. I took charge of the checkbook.

It didn't take us long to see that the seminar leader didn't know anything about what makes productive and meaningful relationships. For me to be in charge of the checkbook was total folly. Within two months, the bills (and just about everything else in dollars and cents) was in total chaos. I eagerly returned the checkbook to Lorraine.

In our confusing attempt at "Christian roles," we completely overlooked the fact that Lorraine was comfortable with the role of bookkeeper and very talented at it. She was the best choice in our family for keeping track of the money that God gave us. She had a college degree in accounting and thoroughly enjoyed keeping the books. I knew absolutely nothing about accounting, and I hated keeping books.

We were trying to force ourselves to operate from a position of weakness. I was supposed to "get strong" in this area. But why? Lorraine was an expert in this and enjoyed it.

To deprive Lorraine of the thing she was good at and enjoyed was ridiculous. We are partners, and properly managing our money is one goal of our relationship. Changing that goal to teaching me to manage the books was not only totally unnecessary but harmful.

Why should I deny Lorraine the opportunity of operating from and exercising her strength? If I were to become strong everywhere that I'm weak, then I wouldn't have much need for relationships.

This may sound almost un-American and can be construed as ungodly by those with preconceived notions about where God intends relationship strengths to be. The Bible makes it clear, however, that we should not expect to be perfect specimens of strength.

"Now the body is not made up of one part but of many.... If the whole body were an eye, where would the sense of hearing be? If the whole body were an ear, where would the sense of smell be?" (1 Cor. 12:14-17)

This passage implies that you can't eliminate your weaknesses. You'll never be able to be all things. So accept that, and identify where you are weak and need the help of others.

The skilled business executive or manager helps other people identify their areas of strength and operates from a position of strength, not weakness. Corporations are put together in a manner that allows people with differing skills and strengths to operate from that perspective. The same is true of other relationships, be it a marriage, business venture, or friendship.

The entire teaching in the Bible about being members of a body (1 Cor. 12:12-31) instructs us to operate from a position of strength. Can you imagine trying to hear through an eye? Many relationships encourage doing just that.

Maintaining a Common Goal

Earlier, in our definition of teamwork, we said a team is two or more people moving along a path of interaction toward a common goal. In preserving a relationship, it is imperative that everybody in the relationship continually focus on this common goal.

In figure 16, we represent a group of people involved in a relationship. The major force holding the relationship together is a common goal. Many things in a relationship tend to pull it apart, and you have to have a goal as a magnet drawing it together.

Note that this magnet is a *common* goal, not just my goal or your goal. Many relationships run out of gas because the goals are set up by just one or two people and then imposed on the rest of the team. When that occurs, you have only a collection of bodies, not a team.

All around us are marriages, families, and businesses where people work together side by side but aren't teams. They don't have common goals.

A classic example is a pastor whom Lorraine and I once knew. We were at his church one Sunday for the "State of the Church Address." We were familiar with what the church was doing and were eager to hear what our friend had to say.

The entire service focused on an explanation of the church's goals. On a large board the pastor had in bold lettering print-

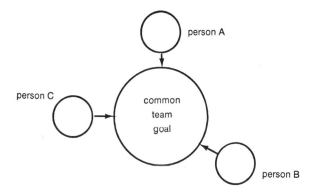

Figure 16. A common team goal is very important to the development and existence of a team. The team goal pulls the individuals together into a common bond. The lack of a common team goal is one of the major reasons for relationship problems within teams or groups of people.

ed several points, summarizing the goals of the church for the coming year.

Halfway through the presentation, Lorraine and I heard some people whispering: Where had the goals come from? We heard it whispered again after the service. We even heard some angry remarks about the goals being "shoved down our throats" from people who previously were instrumental in the support of their pastor.

The sad fact was that our friend, a dynamic, forceful, and motivating leader, presented his own goals to the church. He had violated a fundamental dynamic of a team—*have common goals*. As fine and inspirational as his goals were, they weren't community goals. Though earlier he had been effective in leading that church with a common goal, he now had cut himself off from the community that he was supposed to be leading. We weren't surprised later when we learned that he was no longer ministering at that church.

If your goal is to maintain a cooperative relationship, you must base your relationship on team dynamics. That doesn't mean there aren't times in a state of emergency when you must make decisions without counseling others. I certainly don't encourage that we have relationships by committee. I am simply talking about operating by a value system and not by a political system.

Politics involves a pecking order and the "rights of hierarchy." If we operate our relationships by politics, we end up with a pecking order emphasizing "rights." We develop a class system, with the president parking his car at the closest point to get out of the rain, because he has a "right."

That is the secular approach to relationships. With the modern emphasis on individual rights, some see relationships in terms of "rights" over others. If we are not careful, this attitude could be the downfall of our American system. We must not forget that every time we exercise a right we could be infringing on someone else.

Rights are self-serving and do not advance relationships. Unfortunately, politics, hierarchy, and demanding rights is typical of numerous relationships in which Christians are involved, including the church, the working world, and our own families. We often talk about serving others, but most of us go through life demanding our rights. The Bible teaches that the only basis of relationships is service to others and God. And Jesus became the perfect model of it.

Ownership and Putting Others First

Ownership plays an important role in any team process. The sense of ownership, as well as the feeling that we share in the team's accomplishments, comes from participation in setting a common goal.

We feel much different about goals that we help formulate than about those imposed upon us. The goals we set together are "ours," because we participate in their development.

Therefore, we must promote participation in goal setting, because that provides the ownership needed to develop commitment to the goal.

It is imperative that we learn to think as team members and

not just as individuals. We must consider how our action or lack of it affects everyone else in our relationships and not just how it affects us.

Let me give a crude example. I was the last one out of bed yesterday. By the time I was up, everybody else was gone. I had to go out of town, so I was thinking right away about what I needed to take with me. I dressed and started to leave the room when I noticed the unmade bed.

Unmade beds don't bother me at all. I can walk around an unmade bed, sit on an unmade bed, and casually walk out on an unmade bed. But one thing I know. Unmade beds drive my wife bananas.

I knew Lorraine would be home that afternoon before I got home. I had to make a decision. Either I would make the bed for Lorraine and save her the grief of seeing it unmade, or I would leave it for her to make later.

The decision was one that would affect Lorraine in either case. There was no escaping it.

So, I made the bed. It didn't matter to me if I made the bed, but it mattered to the "team."

I don't care if we're talking about father/son, husband/wife, brother/sister, or neighbor/neighbor. From a biblical standpoint, the goal of the relationships we form should be to meet the needs of people.

Let's review Philippians 2:3-4. "Do nothing out of selfish ambition or vain conceit, but in humility consider others better than yourselves. Each of you should look not only to your own interests, but also to the interests of others."

As Christians, that should be the way we relate to people. The biblical philosophy is that whatever we do, be sure we are serving, because that's how we'll get our needs met. My needs are not in the area of my strengths but of my weaknesses.

To serve others, I should operate for them from my strengths. I should, in turn, let other people operate from their strengths, not focus on correcting their weaknesses. Everything we do in a relationship context should be done from a teamwork viewpoint. We become partners together when one is weak and the other is strong.

Things That Pull Us Apart

It's a basic fact that we are pulled away from relationships when our personal goals in life are in conflict with our team goal. If that situation develops, the relationship is doomed to deterioration.

Rich and Margaret started out with a common goal, but over a period of time, personal goals developed that were in conflict with the team goal. It pulled them apart.

Anytime your personal goal conflicts with the team goal, you'll experience the retaliation, domination, and maybe even isolation styles. This could terminate your relationship.

Another basic team problem develops when one member does not make a direct contribution to the accomplishment of the goal of the team with his gifts, skills, abilities, and other strengths. That can quickly undermine everyone's commitment to a common goal.

A few years ago Lorraine and I decided to plan a family budget. With money coming in and bills to be paid, we needed to give more attention to the details of our finances.

Lorraine is the money expert, but the task fell on me to get the budget outlined. What I put together was from my perspective, and Lorraine didn't see eye to eye on my numbers. Instead of working things out, we let it go. I tried to force the thing through, not making Lorraine a real part of the budget process at any point. I wasn't realistically using her talents and gifts to decide what to buy, when to buy it, and how to organize the payments properly.

As long as I tried by myself to put a budget together, it never worked. It could work only when I got Lorraine's skills and strengths in that area involved.

The third thing that pulls negatively at teamwork: a member lacks the freedom to represent the team. If we actually are members of a team, then we should be at liberty to express the traits of the team we represent. If others in or out of the team try to destroy that freedom in some members of the team, the relationship is undermined. This is true of all our relationships, even the most subtle "unseen" ones.

For instance a few years ago, the typical modern businesswoman almost always wore a certain type of dress suit. Lorraine came home one evening saying she needed one.

It seemed strange to me that this could be so important, but if I wasn't willing to let her "speak" as a member of the businesswoman team, I'd be undermining her relationships as a member. She wanted to speak for and represent her peers on the team, showing that women can have a professional "air" about them as well as men can.

Similarly, I remember the first time Ron came home wearing a necklace. I believed that only squirrely people wear necklaces. And I began harrassing him.

But he needed to wear it, because it represented his belonging to a certain peer group. It was important to him as a teenager.

A fourth thing that can pull us away from teamwork relates to the unwillingness of members to be supportive of one another in other relationships. To be a strong team, we must be willingly supportive of our partners in their roles in other relationships.

There are hundreds more antiteam factors we can't detail because every relationship is unique. Every relationship has its own set of factors at work applying pressure to pull it apart.

However, a relationship will remain strong so long as those involved have an opportunity and are encouraged to use their strengths to meet the needs of others in the team and as long as each team member participates in the development and achievement of the team goal.

10

Communication: How to Share Thoughts and Feelings

When God called Moses to lead His people out of bondage, Moses said, "O Lord, I have never been eloquent.... I am slow of speech and tongue" (Ex. 4:10).

When God called Jeremiah to be a prophet, Jeremiah said, "Ah, Sovereign Lord ... I do not know how to speak" (Jer. 1:6).

Feeling inadequate as a communicator and lacking communication skills is something common to most of us. At my relationships seminars, the number one problem people identify in relationships is poor communication.

Human beings constantly work on the mechanical side of communication—building television sets, video cassettes, and satellite systems. But personal face-to-face communication still causes us great problems.

Every year we leap great hurdles technologically. We can assimilate information in a matter of seconds with computers (now in the home!), and we can send that information at lightning speed.

Yet, technological advances have helped little with personal communication. We have made but little improvement since the days of Moses and Jeremiah in sharing our thoughts and feelings face-to-face with others.

Communication is to a relationship what blood is to the body. If you were to tie a tourniquet around your arm, you would eventually lose the feeling in that arm. It would become dead and useless.

That's exactly what lack of communication does to a relationship. If you start cutting off communication, the relationship deteriorates and then dies. Correct messages about our feelings stop going from one to the other, and we are unable to function as partners.

Therefore, it is imperative that people involved in relationships keep their communication lines open. But to do that we need to develop, learn, and practice effective communication principles.

Defining Communication

If you visit a public library, you will find many volumes written on communication. Entire books are dedicated to simply defining communication.

For our purposes, let's use a one-sentence definition. *Communication is a process that conveys understanding from one person or group to another.*

If we dissect that definition, we come up with two crucial elements. First, communication is a *process.* A sequence of actions and events are involved in establishing good communication.

Second, the purpose of that process is *to develop understanding.* Communication conveys understanding from one person to another, not just words, information, memos, or conversations.

Unless understanding occurs, we really haven't communicated with each other. That is where the problems often exist in communication. Many times we confuse the methodology of communicating with the fact of communicating.

In other words, we think: *I told you something, and now you know it. I sent you a memo, so you understand. I wrote you a letter, so you know what I thought and felt.*

A young couple came to talk with me after a seminar one

day. The wife complained that they had a communication problem. The husband disagreed.

He said, "I don't understand why my wife thinks we have a communication problem. I'm home every day. I *talk* to her every day."

With tears in her eyes, she looked at him and almost yelled, "Yes, but you never listen. You never really hear what I have to say! And you have no idea what I think and how I feel!"

He looked her right in the eyes and said, "What are you talking about? I hear every word. And all you do is talk, talk, talk!"

The husband was confusing conversation with communication. He talked and she talked, but since there was no understanding, they hadn't communicated.

A few years ago, I was project manager of a federal program. One year the Fourth of July came on a Thursday. I decided it would be nice if we all took Friday off too, giving us a four-day weekend.

I asked one of my administrative assistants to inform the staff that we would be taking Friday, July 5 off along with Thursday, July 4. I felt pleased that I had done this good thing.

Well, Friday morning I was enjoying sleeping in when the phone rang. I looked at the clock. It was 7:50.

I answered the phone and the secretary to one of the department heads said, "Mr. Rush, I don't understand what's going on. I'm down here at work and all the doors are locked and nobody is here yet."

"That's right," I said. "Nobody is supposed to be at work today."

She told me no one had informed her, and I told her to go on home and enjoy the free day and the rest of her weekend. After I hung up, I immediately called my administrative assistant and awakened him, angrily chewing him out for not following my instructions. (I had this vision of more people coming to the office and finding things locked up.)

The two of us sat on our beds arguing over the phone about

memos and messages and informing people. "I assure you I told every person that we were taking Friday as well as Thursday off," he said, upset that I was questioning him.

I asked him to tell me specifically what he had done to inform every person, and he said, "Myron, I distinctly remember putting a memo in every department head's box, informing the staffs of the four-day weekend."

He assumed that because he had sent a memo, he had communicated. We later found that the uninformed secretary had failed to pick up her boss' mail that day, as did several other people.

Most people found out through the grapevine that Friday was part of the long holiday weekend, but one secretary went the whole day without hearing a word.

It is important to learn that just using the tools of communication does not guarantee that people understand us.

Let's explore the various aspects of the process of communication to insure that we are not only talking and using the other communication tools, but also developing understanding.

The Master Communicator

Jesus was the Master Communicator. It is quite evident as you read the four Gospels of the New Testament that Jesus was ingenious at communicating the greatest truths of all time. Yet He had none of today's sophisticated technology.

You also see further evidence of Jesus' communication skills when you realize that His message—the divine truth behind His words, actions, and life—comes through all the way down to us today. He communicated in such a way that now, hundreds of years after He spoke, we can read and understand His message.

Jesus could communicate understanding to the individual, to the small group, and to the masses. He could convey His thoughts, feelings, and ideas both to children and to the most educated and sophisticated people of His day.

In Matthew 13, we see Jesus communicating to His disciples

in a small group. Through the use of a series of parables, He explained the kingdom of heaven to them. Afterward, He asked them, "Have you understood all these things?" (v. 51)

The disciples said emphatically, "Yes."

We see that even after using various examples and approaches, Jesus checked to see if He was being understood. We can carry on lengthy conversations but still risk misunderstanding. Jesus put emphasis on understanding, not on brilliance or clever turns of phrases. He wanted people to really know what He was communicating.

Unless we get the same affirmative response that Jesus did when we talk to people, we haven't communicated. We haven't developed understanding.

The Communication Process

Our definition states that communication is a process that conveys understanding. Therefore, if we want to be good communicators, we must know how to apply the process.

There are three aspects to communicating:

The first concerns the sender, or the one we'll call the speaker. The speaker must develop a clear concept of the ideas and feelings he intends to convey and be willing to communicate them. He must choose the right words, actions, or other tools for transmitting his ideas and feelings.

The second aspect concerns both the speaker and the listener. Both must identify and minimize the communication barriers that tend to hamper understanding.

The third aspect concerns the listener. The listener must pay attention to the words or other communication tools and observe the actions of the speaker. He must also have an honest desire to hear what the speaker is saying. Finally, the listener should be able to feed back the thoughts and feelings the speaker has transmitted and be willing to accept the speaker's ideas and feelings without judging them.

The communication process, then, is a two-way street. Both speakers and listeners must use their skills in order to develop understanding.

In this chapter, we will discuss the steps that the speaker takes in his part of the communication process. In the next chapter, we will examine the barriers to good communication, and consider the listener's part in the communication process.

Step One

All understanding begins with the speaker. Unless we come up with a clear concept in our own minds of the ideas and feelings we have, it will be impossible for us to communicate understanding to someone else.

Clarifying our concepts is the first step—and the first big problem—in communicating.

Not long ago my daughter went stomping through the house obviously upset. When I approached her to find out what the problem was, she angrily replied that she was upset with her brother.

When I asked her why, she said, "Just because."

"Just because" told me nothing. I didn't understand why she was angry. I didn't understand what her thoughts and feelings were.

So many people go through relationships communicating "just because" statements. That leaves everything open to misunderstanding. Delphine was really telling me she didn't want me to know what had her so upset.

The hardest step in the communication process is for us to share honestly, "Here's what I think, and here's what I feel."

It is so difficult because if I do tell you what I really think or feel and you reject my thoughts or feelings, then you have rejected me. Nobody wants to be rejected. And sometimes we have reason to feel we will be. So we play silly word games. We communicate something that is not so threatening.

Sometimes we'll reveal just a small portion of our true thoughts and feelings and watch how others receive it. If they are receptive, then we'll open up a bit more. If they reject us on that little bit, we retreat, afraid of further rejection.

Unless we share our thoughts and feelings honestly, we can never maintain true communication in our relationships. That means we have three alternatives in honestly revealing ourselves. We can trust the other person not to reject us, and therefore speak openly. We can speak openly even though we fear rejection, because the risk of alienation is preferable to broken communication. Or we can hold back, "playing safe" in the relationship but actually limiting it.

To illustrate how we frequently fail to express our true thoughts and feelings, let me tell you about a communication problem Lorraine and I had over our jeep truck.

Recently, I had our four-wheel drive Jeep repainted. Before I did, I discussed color options with Lorraine to see what she would like. She said, "I don't care, Myron. Paint it whatever color you want."

I picked green and white, because that's what I wanted.

When I picked it up at the shop with Lorraine, she saw it and gasped, "Oh, what a terrible color!"

I became angry and replied, "Why didn't you say something about the color before?"

We argued all the way home. She thought a two-tone brown would have been better. We went around and around about my poor choice.

Sometime before this, Lorraine and I were in a shopping mall. We paused at a dress shop window and she said, "Look at that dress, Myron."

I looked at it, and I figured maybe she wanted the dress, so I said, "Oh, yeah, I think it would look nice on you."

She went in and tried on the dress and said, "What do you think?"

It wasn't that great of a dress, but what do I know? Assuming she wanted to buy it, I gave my approval. "I think you ought to get it, Lorraine."

She brought the dress home, wore it once, and then let it hang in her closet for weeks. One morning as we were getting ready for church, I said, "Hey, Lorraine, why don't you wear that new dress you bought?"

She said a little hesitantly, "Oh, I really don't like the color."

I was totally confused, and asked her why she bought it. She said she thought I liked it on her.

The two of us had stood in front of that dress shop looking at a dress neither of us liked that much. Without saying what we really thought or felt, we bought it!

Purchasing the dress was no serious thing, and it caused no problems in our relationship (a few laughs but no problems). However, when we make a habit of not telling our partners how we really think or feel, it becomes impossible for needs to be met in the relationship.

Therefore, be willing to communicate your true thoughts and feelings. This is essential for developing understanding within the relationship.

Recently I was conducting a management training program for a group of nurses in a hospital. After one of the sessions, the head nurse came to me and asked if I was aware that one of the nurses believed I was trying to get her fired.

We'd been conducting the program for six months, but I had no idea what she was talking about. I was flabbergasted. "Why would I want to get her fired?" I asked the head nurse.

She didn't know. She was apologetic about bringing it up and said she was just as embarrassed as I, but she felt I should know how this nurse felt.

When that day's session was over, I walked down the hall with the nurse who believed I was trying to get her fired. When I asked if I could buy her a cup of coffee, she was reluctant but with some encouragement finally agreed.

When we sat down with our coffee, I immediately confronted her with the problem I'd heard about and told her I wanted to resolve it.

At first, she denied it, insisting there was nothing wrong. But she finally got it out in the open. She told me I must be trying to get her fired because my illustrations of poor nursing practices fit her personally. She was sure I was talking about her, because she had done some of the things I criticized.

I assured her I did not know about her or her practices and

in a matter of minutes we resolved the entire problem.

Countless relationship problems never have a chance to be resolved. Two things happened to help this particular relationship problem.

First, the head nurse had the foresight and courage to tell me about the problem and urge me to do something about it.

Second, I was willing to confront the nurse concerning a misunderstanding that I thought she had about me.

So many times people having a relationship problem go to someone completely outside of the relationship. Others talk about it, turning the problem into juicy gossip, while the relationship still flounders. Seldom do outsiders who know what's going on try to resolve relationship problems with the people involved. Fortunately, the head nurse did.

Another disaster results when people who actually have the problem don't confront their partners with the issue. Many times after a seminar, people come to me with all sorts of relationship problems. But they won't talk with the person with whom they are having the problem. I can listen, but they need to talk with their partner about it to really resolve the matter.

Step Two

Once a speaker of a message gets a clear understanding of his own thoughts and feelings and is willing to communicate them, the next step calls for selecting appropriate words and actions to convey those thoughts and feelings.

This brings up another problem with communication. "Words don't have any meaning. People have meaning for words." I've heard that all my life. And it's true.

The English language has many words that can mean several things at one time. We can't depend on words alone to carry our messages. We have to consider how we use the words, and we have to check to see if they are understood.

For example, take the word "strike." It's a very common word. But it has a variety of uses and meanings in everyday conversation. We strike a match to ignite it. When labor unions strike, they stop working. If we strike a ball, we hit it; but if we miss a ball, that's a strike too. A baseball player doesn't want to get strikes, but a bowler is ecstatic over them.

We recognize that the use of the word strike fits into different settings. The baseball player, the union leader, and the bowler all have "communication systems" with special meanings for some of the same words.

Incredibly, on July 20, 1969 we placed the first American on the moon.

Not long ago at a seminar on the West Coast, I talked with one of the engineers involved in the project. As we discussed the importance of communication, he said, "When we put together the space project, we had millions of people working on thousands of interrelated projects literally around the world. If we hadn't come up with an efficient communication system, we would never have reached our goals.

"Part of my job," he said, "was to help devise the simplest yet most effective communication system for all of those projects."

He and his staff came up with a simple system of relatively few words that could each have only one meaning. The basic principle was to have a clear meaning that could not be confused in the fast-paced situations in which they were trying to work.

We don't live in such sterile communication modes, but the point is clear. We can't depend on words to do the whole job of communicating our thoughts and feelings. We have to be sure our audience understands the meanings we are giving those words.

Not long ago my daughter brought home a definition of "memory" from her college class. It is astoundingly confusing. Here she is, studying under a professor with a doctor's degree in communication and he hands out the worse possible collection of words to explain what he means.

When Delphine came home complaining that the professor used such giant words she couldn't understand what he was trying to communicate, I told her she just needed to get the meaning of the words clear and then she would be all right. She handed me the definition in exasperation and asked if I could understand it.

It said, "As related to learning, memory is the storage and retrieval of the relatively stable potential for subsequent occurrence of the response."

After reading that thing over about ten times, I still had no idea what he was saying.

It seems the more educated we get, the more problems we have communicating. We tend to pick $64 words that other people either don't understand or can interpret in a multitude of ways.

Over the years, our use of the English language has tended to evolve from the simple to the complex. For example, the Lord's Prayer has only 52 words in the *New International Version* of the Bible. Lincoln's Gettysburg address has only 268 words. The Declaration of Independence, a document meant to establish a nation, has only 1,322 words.

By contrast, a recent government document on the vital matter of selling cabbage contains 26,901 words. You may think you know what cabbage is, but after reading just a part of this you will begin to wonder.

When the Apostle Paul came to the people of Corinth, he said, "I did not come with eloquence or superior wisdom as I proclaimed to you the testimony about God (1 Cor. 2:1).

Paul was educated enough to use lofty words and brilliant ideas. He was a learned man. Since Corinth was one of the cultural centers of Greece and the world, it seems logical that Paul would try to impress the people with great rhetoric.

He didn't do that. He realized the importance of keeping communication simple.

Recently I joined Jerry, a friend of mine, in doing a "fog index" on the latest IRS instruction booklet for filling out personal income tax returns. A fog index is a formula for adding up words in a sentence and dividing them by their range of difficulty. The higher the rating, the "foggier" and more useless the writing becomes.

The IRS claims anyone can fill out his taxes by using the instructions attached to the forms. Jerry and I took a paragraph at random and it came out at a 39 rating.

The figure refers to the number of years in school needed to understand what is being said. A scholar with a Ph.D. may have some twenty-six years of study. This IRS paragraph required thirteen years beyond that in order for a reader to easily grasp its meaning.

According to studies, nobody really operates in daily communication levels much beyond the sixth-grade level. It's just easier to communicate at that level.

Managers of businesses are so busy and tormented by paperwork that they read at about an eighth-grade level. That doesn't mean that managers are poorly educated. It means they need to understand things quickly and easily in their busy schedules.

We can't expect people to operate at high levels of understanding in normal everyday conversation. College statistics tell us we can't expect people to operate at high levels of understanding even in academic situations.

When I was director of Alaskan students higher education in Anchorage, we tested all incoming freshmen. The average student was reading at the sixth-grade level. Their verbal communication was much the same.

The professors were not only assigning reading at college level, but they were talking at that level too. It's no wonder freshmen so often failed in their first year at school. They couldn't understand what they were reading or what was being said to them.

Some people are geared more to talking than to reading, but the problems are no different. We use thousands of words every day and assume that people understand what we mean by the words we use.

For example, in 24 hours, Americans make 679 million telephone calls, and 50 million long distance calls. Talking has become a way of life, even if we can't be face-to-face with each other.

One of the keys to effective communication is in the words we select to convey our thoughts and feelings.

Before we ever speak, we should try to make sure we are using the language of the listener. That means we must use words that are familiar to others and attach only those meanings to words that our listeners will understand.

Words and Actions

The nonverbal communication of a speaker is often more important than the words he uses. Numerous studies conducted by communication specialists show that many ideas, thoughts, and feelings are communicated nonverbally.

What this means is that we communicate a great deal by our body movements or actions.

Albert Mehrabian, a communication reseacher, discovered that as much as 55 percent of a message we send may be communicated nonverbally through actions. Another 38 percent of a message may be communicated through tone of voice. That leaves only 7 percent communicated through spoken words.

Tone and actions may convey up to 93 percent of our thoughts and feelings to the people with whom we communicate. The speaker of a message must be aware of this in order to use the right actions to support his words.

We must keep in mind that communication is a two-way street involving a *sender* and *receiver* (or a talker and a listener).

To be good communicators, we must not only learn how to state what we really think and feel effectively, but we must also learn how to listen effectively.

Next, let's focus on the keys to becoming a good listener.

11

Learning to Be a Perceptive Listener

A few years ago, Lorraine and I bought a new house and started through all of the exciting discussions that occurs when a family makes such a purchase.

We picked out carpets, interior color combinations, the exterior color, lamps, and much more. All the planning started to get exhausting after awhile; I longed for the day we could live in it.

Finally, a few months later the house was finished. We were anxious to move in. In fact, while people were still cleaning up after the carpet installers, we were already dragging in our furniture. When we looked around, we realized that in our rush we had forgotten one thing—the drapes.

After we were somewhat settled, Lorraine started planning for the drapes. She was still full of energy. She went down to a drapery store and brought home huge sample books of hundreds and hundreds of fabric possibilities. Soon they were strewn all over the floor of the living room.

I was almost burned out on house planning, but Lorraine kept at it. She kept asking me how this one looked and that one looked. After awhile they all looked the same to me.

The drapes ended up being the most difficult choice we made. This routine of fabric books on the floor, and discussing possible combinations continued for days.

I would come home from work to be met by Lorraine holding a drapery sample. I'd pick my way through the piles of sample books to put down my jacket. Then all through dinner we would have lengthy discussions about this drape and that drape.

I was totally blurred by it all. I started tuning out the whole thing. When Lorraine would talk drapes, I would think about where I could go fishing the next weekend. I stopped listening to her.

One afternoon I came home from work and the sample books were all gone. The floor was clean. On the walls were hanging crisp new drapes. I stared at them and said, "Lorraine! When did you decide on these?"

Lorraine was in the kitchen. There was a moment of awful silence and then a pan slammed. Lorraine came up to me and almost shouted, "What do you mean, when did *I* decide on these? You were the one who told me that was the color to choose," she said, pointing at a drape that I was sure I'd never seen before in my life.

"You weren't even listening when we picked it, were you?" she said, seeing my confused look.

It was true. I had been nodding in agreement at anything she said about the drapes. I didn't even know she'd asked me about the final design and color.

Throughout my marriage and my relationship with employees, employers, and friends, I've too often found myself in similar situations. I discover too late that I failed to listen to what was being said to me. Yet I pretended to be listening, creating big problems.

As I conduct seminars on relationships around the country, I find I'm not alone. Most of us have similar problems, with our spouses, children, fellow workers, and friends.

Recently, at the end of one seminar, a young man complained to me that his boss regularly rejected all of his ideas.

He said he had recently come up with what he thought was a solution to an inventory control problem in the Accounting

Department. As he shared this potential solution with me, I said, "Hey, you ought to go to your boss and tell him about it. You shouldn't be talking to me."

He frowned. "No use going to my boss. He never listens to what I say. He just tunes me out."

The ability to be a good listener is one of the major keys to maintaining a cooperative relationship style. I have never seen poor listeners be able to maintain cooperation in their relationships very long, and it's something I've really had to work on to overcome.

The Importance of Listening
Listening is the key to developing understanding.

When I first got into the consulting business, I assumed that the key to good communication was one's ability to verbalize his thoughts and feelings. Over the years, I've changed my thinking. I now believe that the key is the ability to be a good listener.

People interested in improving their communication skills must focus on improving their listening skills. In this chapter, we'll discuss how to be a good listener in order to maintain cooperative relationships.

Another reason listening is so important to relationships is that through listening we identify each other's needs. You may be trying to communicate your needs to me, but if I'm not a good listener I'll never hear you.

Since cooperative relationships are built around our meeting needs for each other, we must all be good listeners to understand each other's needs.

Two Types of Listening
There are two types of listening: one we will call *perceptive* listening and the other, *passive* listening.

Perceptive listening is a process. The receiver attempts to identify and understand the feelings, attitudes, and meaning behind the words or messsage he receives from the sender. Perceptive listening is going beyond just the words and nonverbal messages. It focuses on listening for the thoughts and feelings behind the words and actions.

Passive listening, on the other hand, is a fixed state. The receiver relies solely on what he hears to develop understanding. Passive listening usually leads to misunderstanding because it misses most of the real meaning behind the spoken words.

The Bible gives us a classic case study of the need to use perceptive listening instead of passive listening.

Jesus and His disciples were crossing a lake in a boat. Rocking about in the water, with the waves lapping against the sides of the boat, Jesus began discussing the spiritual hypocrisy of the Pharisees.

He said, "Watch out for the yeast of the Pharisees" (Mark 8:15).

It was a nice day, and the disciples were calmly taking in the weather when they heard Jesus say something about bread.

They started mumbling about bread, and realized they had only one loaf with them. They assumed Jesus was reprimanding them for not preparing properly. This had happened before, and Jesus ended up performing a miracle.

Jesus overheard them talking and asked why they were discussing bread. He said that was irrelevant to what He was saying.

"Do you still not see or understand?" He asked them.

Jesus was trying to teach them spiritual truth. But because they were listening only to His words, they missed the point.

The disciples were listening passively. They picked up a word that set them off on a tangent that was far removed from what Jesus was talking about.

Passive listening commonly leads to misunderstanding. In the previous chapter, we mentioned that only 7 percent of our ideas and feelings may be communicated in the words we use, while 93 percent may be in the various types of nonverbal communication that must be perceived other than through words alone.

Jesus spent a great deal of His ministry trying to teach the disciples how to be perceptive listeners. He knew most of the meaning and understanding is hidden behind the words we use. It is a basic principle of communication.

Misperceptions

Mark Rogers was an ambitious young certified public accountant working for a large accounting firm. When I met Mark, he was a very frustrated man. One day over a cup of coffee he shared how he was convinced that his boss thought him incompetent.

He said, "I'd quit my job in a minute and move to another city if my wife didn't like this town so much. But for her sake, I'll stick it out."

Mark told me that until a few months prior to our discussion he had been working on some of his firm's largest accounts. But slowly over the months his boss for some unexplained reason had taken him off these accounts, putting him instead on small local jobs.

Mark interpreted this as a lack of trust. He thought his boss didn't consider him capable of working on the important accounts.

I asked Mark if he had ever discussed the problem with his boss.

"I tried to, but the only explanation I got was that he thought I needed a change," Mark said. "That tells me he means I can't be trusted to do the work."

I happen to be a personal friend of Mark's boss, and one evening at a party I asked him how Mark was doing at his job.

He told me that Mark was the rising young star in the firm. He said Mark was an energetic, enthusiastic, and competent young accountant and was sure to go far in the company. It was exactly the opposite of what Mark thought.

When I saw Mark, I told him he really should talk to his boss. I explained that there was a great deal of misunderstanding on his part about his boss' feelings. Mark finally agreed.

Later, Mark told me that when he confronted his boss, he

was told that he had been working too hard and getting over extended. His boss wanted to lighten his load a bit so he didn't get career burnout.

Mark could have avoided all the frustration he felt if he had gone through the communication process and taken the time to discover the real meaning behind his boss' words at that first meeting. And likely the boss could have communicated better!

Developing Perceptive Listening Skills

Both my friend Mark and the Apostles in the boat with Jesus should have followed the perceptive listening process as outlined here:

The first step in perceptive listening is to listen for ideas and feelings behind the spoken words. In the previous chapter, we pointed out that most people are reluctant to share their true feelings and ideas unless they have a very strong trust relationship with the people to whom they're talking. As a result, they camouflage what they really think and how they really feel behind the words they speak.

Yes, a perceptive listener will wade through all the words and listen for the ideas and feelings.

The Apostle Paul provides us with a good example of a perceptive listener. Paul traveled to Athens, a city known for its philosophical thinking and its broad conglomeration of religious thought.

One day while he discussed the true God with the men of Athens, he said, "I see that in every way you are very religious" (Acts 17:22).

Paul knew they were religious, not because they told him in so many words, but because he listened to their discussions, observed their shrines, and attended their public debates. By using perceptive listening, he heard the true thoughts and feelings behind their words and actions.

It would have been easy to travel through Athens in Paul's day and conclude that the people were very artistic. They exhibited handiwork in their buildings, statues, and shrines.

But Paul picked up on something more basic. He listened for thoughts, feelings, and ideas, and discovered the true meaning behind the daily discussion of philosophy and religion in the meeting places of Athens.

Later, back in Jerusalem, Paul was arrested and put on trial before the Sanhedrin. The charge was that he had brought Greeks into the Jewish temple, had defiled the holy place, and had taught people against the religious laws.

As the trial progressed, Paul perceived that there was a very near split in the jury. Some members of the jury were Sadducees and the others were Pharisees.

He called out, "My brothers, I am a Pharisee, the son of a Pharisee. I stand on trial because of my hope in the resurrection of the dead" (Acts 23:6).

In those two sentences, Paul captured the essence of disagreement between the Sadducees and Pharisees and pictured himself a victim of their disagreement. He knew that the Sadducees did not believe it possible to be raised from the dead, but the Pharisees did.

Through his perceptive listening, Paul recognized the conditions and issues present among the jury members. The parties didn't wear different clothing. He had to listen intently to the meaning behind their words to know that they represented two conflicting views.

Paul's comments threw the jury into chaos. They began arguing over a completely different issue than the one for which Paul was being tried. "There was a great uproar and some of the teachers of the Law who were Pharisees stood up and argued vigorously. 'We find nothing wrong with this man'" (v. 9).

This is an example of the power of perceptive listening. It can be used to great advantage. Paul was involved in an emotionally charged situation when he was on trial. It was a tense and volatile group. Paul had even been hit in the mouth by someone before he made his statement about being a Pharisee.

Most of us tend to let our emotions overpower us in emotionally charged situations. Paul held his cool, and perceived the underlying thoughts and feelings of others in the situation.

The Second Step

Our second step as listeners is to have an honest desire to hear what the speaker is saying. Much of the confusion and misunderstanding that occurs in communication comes from listeners not being interested in hearing what the speaker has to say.

For example, when Lorraine was trying to pick out drapes, and showed me hundreds of different possibilities, I eventually became uninterested in drape colors and fabrics. I stopped listening.

You cannot be a good listener and establish understanding unless you have an honest desire to hear the speaker.

I believe it is the listener's obligation and responsibility to communicate to the speaker the honest desire, "Keep talking. I want to hear you."

Give the speaker your undivided attention by eye contact. Have you ever noticed the more eye contact you give people the more they share what is on their minds?

Not long ago Lorraine and I were vacationing on the West Coast. One evening we had dinner at a nice restaurant overlooking the California coastline. Though I enjoy living in the Colorado mountains, I appreciate every opportunity I have to admire our nation's beautiful open coastlines. It was a gorgeous evening and I was soaking up the view, only halfheartedly listening to Lorraine.

She was trying to share with me her concerns for an aunt just admitted to the hospital. I have to confess that as long as I heard the sound of her voice, I felt I could inject an "uh-huh" every now and then and still soak up the view.

My real interest was in the sunset.

After awhile, it occurred to me that Lorraine had stopped talking. I turned from the picturesque view to find her glaring at me. "You haven't been listening to one word I've been saying," she charged.

She was right. I didn't want her to know she was right, though, so I said, "Oh, yes, I have. Tell me about your aunt."

She said, "I've been trying to, but you're just not interested.

My failure to give her my undivided attention communicated my lack of interest in what she had to say. Lorraine is a perceptive listener and picked up on my true feelings. She could tell my interest lay where my attention was—out the window.

It is important for the perceptive listener to give the speaker his undivided attention. This will communicate to the sender, "I really do want to hear your thoughts and feelings."

The Third Step

The third step to perceptive listening: when you have listened, feed back certain details to assure the sender you have heard correctly, and the sender will be responsible to say so if you have not.

However, this third step has an additional part to it. When you feed back a thought or feeling to the sender, you must do so without making any judgment on what the speaker is saying. To quickly judge the validity of people's ideas and feelings can force them to deny their feelings or ideas, and justify them in refusing to communicate.

Quick judgment, either for or against what a person says, harms communication. You may be giving blessing to something that a person doesn't have a right to say. Or you may be judging the information unjustly.

Don't be too quick to sanction or criticize a person's thoughts or feelings. Instead say, "Hey, here's what I hear," without assuming it to be right or wrong, good or bad.

It's easy to get into trouble here. Often we begin sending back strange messages of blessing or criticism when we have no intention of doing so.

For example, suppose you're in a conversation with a friend, and you sense a great deal of anger. You might feed that anger back to the sender by saying, "Hey, Charlie, it sounds to me like you're angry at me *again!*"

What are you telling Charlie? You're probably communicating disapproval of his feelings. Remember in the last chapter we said that if people start to reveal to you what they're really thinking and feeling, and then you reject it, they will retreat and hold back their true thoughts and feelings.

It takes special awareness on our part to send back only the ideas and feelings heard, without attaching any interpretation of good or bad.

When Charlie seems angry with you, react instead with, "Sounds to me like you are upset and angry, Charlie." Don't communicate "again," or wrinkle your brow. Just convey what you are hearing.

Jesus was the Master Communicator. It was His art of communication and His thorough understanding of the communication process that enabled Him to train twelve men in three short years to become the leadership core of His worldwide church.

On a regular basis throughout His ministry, Jesus taught the disciples and solicited feedback to determine if they really understood what He was saying to them.

For example, Jesus once carried on a conversation with the disciples about His identity. He asked, "Who do the crowds say I am?" (Luke 9:18, NIV)

Why was Jesus even asking the qustion? He Himself certainly knew his identity. He asked to solicit feedback from the disciples to see how much they understood of all that He had been communicating to them.

Without feedback it is impossible to know if we are communicating. When you think you hear a thought or a feeling, feed it back. Only then will you really know what is said.

When you feed back the ideas and feelings you heard from the sender, he is going to react in agreement or disagreement. He will either confirm or deny what you send back.

For example, Charlie may say, "You're right, Myron. I am angry, and here's why."

He will then have the opportunity to vent the cause of his anger and broaden the base of understanding.

That's the agreement possibility.

Or he may say, "Oh, no, Myron. I'm not angry. I was just kidding."

That's the disagreement possibility, and it can tell you one of two things: Either you did not correctly hear the ideas and feelings, or Charlie isn't comfortable about discussing the feeling with you. He may not trust you with his real ideas and feelings, so he tries to cover them up.

If the latter is the case, never try to force the issue. If you are talking with Charlie and think you hear anger, you should feed it back. But if he denies what you thought you heard, you should accept his denial.

Don't say, "Oh, come on, Charlie. You are angry. Admit it. I've seen that look before."

That is not accepting what Charlie says. If you take that position, what will happen? You will probably drive Charlie further away, and he will become more and more defensive. Your chances of understanding become less and less.

We should never try to force the issue until the person is willing to share his ideas and feelings with us.

Charlie must learn to trust us with his feelings of anger before he will open up and share how he really feels, and why. Therefore, the listener's job is not to force the issue at this point, but to work on strengthening the trust aspect of the relationship.

Once a person feels he can trust you with his true thoughts and feelings, he will be more willing to share them.

The Rules of Proper Listening

There are four important rules to follow to be an effective listener:

1. Don't interrupt the speaker.

2. Don't start forming your response while the speaker is still talking.

3. Do ask questions for clarity.

4. Don't assume you already know what the speaker is going to say.

One of the most common mistakes listeners make is interrupting a speaker. Scripture says there is "a time to keep silent, and a time to speak."

This certainly is one of the most important principles of listening. All of us need to learn when to keep silent and should begin by attacking the practice of interrupting a speaker.

A few years ago when I was working as a personnel director, a member of my staff came to work one Monday morning and I gave him a traditional greeting. "How are you doing today, Frank?"

He gave me a traditional meaningless response. "Oh, fine. How are you?"

But there was something about his tone and the look on his face that communicated that he really wasn't fine. I invited Frank into my office for coffee.

I explained to him that I wasn't trying to be nosy, but he appeared to me not to be "fine." I said he had the opportunity to talk if he felt he had something he wanted to discuss with me.

I was a personnel director, and this was part of my job. But Frank was more than just an employee. He was also a friend, whose family was very close to mine. I really wanted to help, but I was not prepared for what followed. Because of our friendship, Frank told me all about what was troubling him.

I was quite shocked to hear that over the weekend his wife had kicked him out of the house, was filing for divorce, and had issued a restraining order prohibiting him from going to the house to see his children.

As Frank talked, a multitude of questions came to my mind. I found myself interrupting him with them. I was not following the first rule of being an effective, perceptive listener.

My interruptions confused Frank's train of thought, making it more difficult for me to understand his true thoughts and feelings.

I broke the second rule too. I found myself formulating my responses to Frank's news. What advice could I give him?

What should I say to help the guy out?

Each time I went through the mental exercise of trying to think of something inspiring to say, I missed something Frank was saying to me. Then I would interrupt him again to ask what he had just said, throwing him off his train of thought again.

I felt that I was following the clarification rule. I asked him several times to repeat certain things to me, not to be sure I understood but because I simply wasn't listening properly. I was busy trying to think of things to say in response to the shocking things I was hearing.

The longer we talked, the more emotionally involved I became. I was closer to Frank than to his wife, and I began to sanction what he was saying, taking his side. I even began to pass judgment on his wife, contrary to what I have described as the third step toward being a perceptive listener.

As I said, initially I was at least keeping the rule of trying to clarify what Frank was saying, but because I got involved in making judgments, I eventually broke that rule too. I was so wrapped up in what he was saying, I didn't feel that I should keep asking him questions. However, I wasn't listening well enough to know what he was saying. Consequently, I broke the fourth rule to effective listening. I assumed that I knew what he was saying.

The longer we talked, the more I found myself assuming that I knew what Frank would tell me next.

This is a very common misunderstanding of listeners. We should never assume we know what the speaker is going to say. When we do, we start interpreting words to fit our assumption.

Eventually, I found myself interrupting Frank and saying, "I know what you mean." Yet I had no idea what he was feeling. I was lost to what was really happening in our communication process.

Frank spent over an hour telling me what he thought and how he felt, only because I took the initiative to solicit his true thoughts and feelings. But I wasn't prepared. I missed his real thoughts and feelings because I broke most of the rules of communication and listening.

Barriers to Communication

In the previous chapter we mentioned that between the message sent by the speaker and what is heard by the listener there exists some barriers to communication.

In order for understanding to be complete, it is important that both the speaker and the listener be aware of the communication barriers between them and the potential effect on the communication process.

As I conduct seminars around the country, I usually ask participants to identify the major communication barriers they experience while communicating. The four most common are:

1. My own unmet personal needs
2. Conflicting ideas and feelings
3. Personal prejudices
4. Premature assumptions

Personal needs become a major barrier in the communication process. As we elaborated throughout this book, our needs get our attention. It is very difficult for me to listen to your needs and give them attention when I have an unmet need of my own.

Therefore, unmet personal needs tend to become a distraction.

A second barrier consists of conflicting ideas and feelings. As you share your ideas and feelings with me, my thoughts and feelings can conflict with yours. It becomes very difficult for me to accept your thoughts and feelings when I disagree with them.

Third, our prejudices tend to distort our understanding. Whenever I do management consultant work with Christian organizations, they always ask me what church I attend.

They want to exercise their prejudices right out front, to figure out what my doctrine is before they even hear me. All of us have built in prejudices like this. We think, *Oh, he's a Methodist.* Or, *Ah, a Catholic.* Or, *Uh-huh, a Baptist.* We have mental images of what these people are, images that can distort how we hear and understand their thoughts and feelings.

Lastly, in the list of top four barriers to communication, we tend to make too many assumptions about what people think, feel, and mean when we hear them talking. We greatly increase the risk of misunderstanding, because we want to be quick of mind and capable to using our vast experience to grasp instantly what is happening around us.

The important thing about these and other communication barriers is to recognize their existence. Then we can work on minimizing their effect.

They do exist. We can't eliminate them. We must realize they are there and work with them to improve our understanding.

Proverbs 18:13 states, "He who answers before listening—that is his folly and his shame." This verse speaks to the importance of perceptive listening in the communication process. If we don't want to experience folly and shame, listening is essential.

12

The Role Commitment Plays in Relationships

Relationships are no stronger than the commitment we make to them. Consider the friendship of David and Jonathan described in Scripture.

"Jonathan became one in spirit with David, and he loved him as himself" (1 Sam. 18:1). You can't be more committed than that.

Later Jonathan had to say good-bye to David, but the result of their friendship was to be felt for centuries to come. "Go in peace, for we have sworn friendship with each other in the name of the Lord, saying, 'The Lord is witness between you and me, and between your descendants and my descendants forever'" (1 Sam. 20:42).

These two friends had an extremely strong commitment, the kind that brings a lump to your throat. They expected their good relationship to extend even to their descendants. That expectation was not unrealistic. Nor is it a possibility only for biblical characters. They were also humans.

Regardless of problems, pain, and separation, David and Jonathan made a strong commitment to each other. As you continue to read 1 Samuel, you find their commitment so strong that they risked their lives for each other. There aren't many relationships like that today. We expect our partners in relationships to always act cooperatively. When they let us down, we let them down too.

But even if our relationships lack in performance from others, we should not let down on our commitment. Even if our commitment must last an entire lifetime without response.

Right after graduation from high school, I worked in heavy construction as an equipment operator for a boss named Frank. He was a heavy drinker, got into barroom fights at least once a week, and was known to beat his wife occasionally. I was actually afraid of Frank. Most people who worked for him were. He had a violent temper, and in arguments went after people, with little concern that either he or someone else might be killed. I saw him pick up a hammer once and throw it at workers when they didn't follow his instructions. Frank was simply a mean man.

I worked for Frank for almost three years before deciding to go back to college. During that time, one person continually puzzled me by the way she remained totally committed to this brutish man. It was his wife, Helen.

When I was working for Frank, Lorraine and I were newlyweds. We were shocked that this kind of relationship even existed between people. Helen stayed with Frank no matter what he did to embarrass her, hurt her, or cheat on her.

One weekend, Helen and Frank had their twenty-fifth wedding anniversary, and we were invited to the party. As we drove home afterward, Lorraine and I discussed how amazed we were at Helen. She was a sweet, soft-spoken, extremely attractive middle-aged woman—with a louse of a husband.

Lorraine said she had talked with Helen that afternoon. She had asked how Helen had achieved this major accomplishment—over twenty-five years to remain with a man that most people knew to be a terror.

Helen had replied, "When I said 'I do' twenty-five years ago, I made that commitment for life."

She told Lorraine that she hadn't said, "I do, if. . . ." Her commitment was made regardless of the circumstances, not only if they went her way.

She said, "If I live long enough, I expect to celebrate my fiftieth anniversary with this man."

Helen didn't have to do that. About five years later, Frank was killed in a car wreck while driving home drunk from a tavern.

Every time I think of commitment in relationships, I'm reminded of her. Frank never changed his behavior, or his style of physical relationships. Helen didn't either.

Unfortunately, today we are living in a society where commitment in relationships carries little longevity but lots of conditions. Most people are willing to commit only to those things that meet their personal needs.

We are almost taught that another's needs are another's problems. Society is very unsupportive of long term commitments, especially when they require sacrifice.

But commitment is the mortar of relationships. Without that cementing of people, relationships don't last or meet other's needs.

The only way to maintain cooperative relationships over the long road is by making strong commitments.

In this final chapter, we will look at the impact that commitment has on binding relationships together, as well as the types of commitment needed to maintain cooperation on a continuing basis.

We also will see that if we are going to implement the principles of this book, we need to be committed to God and His principles for maintaining cooperative relationships.

Until now, we've talked about what needs to be done according to God's principles. The danger is that we may stop here, with only an intellectual grasp of the cycle of relationships—why they deteriorate or why they improve.

One can understand the entire relationship cycle and be familiar with the various tools needed to maintain a cooperative relationship and still do nothing.

Unless we are willing to make a commitment to our relationships, all this information becomes only "head knowledge," and we'll never translate it into action.

Commitment in a Cooperation Style Relationship

The commitments we make must focus on the other person and not on ourselves.

I recently read a biography of one of Hollywood's leading film stars. In one chapter, she discusses her many marriages. She had just left her seventh husband and was preparing for her eighth when the interviewer asked her to sum up why she had so many men in her life.

She said matter-of-factly, "In all my marriages, I found myself eventually getting bored."

She saw all seven of those commitments totally in terms of herself. She was committed to *exciting men*, not to a lasting relationship with a husband. When boredom set in, her commitment required that she get another exciting man.

In order to have a lasting relationship that becomes, in terms of this book, an ongoing cooperative relationship, it is imperative that we be committed to meeting the needs of the other people we relate to and not to something in ourselves.

Unless we are willing to make such commitments to the others involved in the relationship, we'll find it impossible to establish long-term cooperative relationships with anyone.

The best we could hope for would be a one-sided relationship like that of Frank and Helen, where a Helen would commit to us. Not making long term commitments ourselves makes us totally dependent on others to make the long-term commitments.

Everyone Must Have Commitment

In a cooperative relationship, each partner is committed to the other person. This means there is mutual commitment—it is not one-sided.

Frequently at seminars, I run into teary-eyed wives with husbands who no longer meet their needs. I meet depressed and dejected husbands who wonder why their wives don't love them anymore. I meet exhausted people who are frustrated, hurt, and angry about their jobs. I meet people who have lost lifelong friends over an argument.

At a recent seminar, Lorraine and I met a young woman who attached herself to Lorraine. During every coffee break, and at lunch time, she bemoaned the fact that she was deeply in love with a young man and highly committed to him, but he didn't love her. They weren't married, because he didn't want to get married. He wanted to be a friend, and that was all.

She told Lorraine she had proposed marriage to him, but he wouldn't agree to a trip to the altar. Her dilemma, she said, was that he was not willing to make the same commitment to her that she was willing to make (and actually said she already had made) to him.

At every opportunity, she pressed Lorraine to tell her what she could do to get this guy to marry her. Lorraine tried to point out to her that unless there was mutual commitment, the relationship was impossible. She wasn't going to be able to form a cooperative relationship with someone all by herself. She finally advised her not to pursue the relationship unless this commitment could be developed.

This is a relationship that never got started because the two people never really shared any mutual commitments. But the majority of people we talk with have relationships that have gone on the rocks.

Often, Lorraine and I hear, "Oh, I'm keeping my commitment, and I'm still meeting his needs. But he's not meeting mine anymore. What do I do?"

In recent years, we've been hearing the same refrain from many men about their wives.

The same is true in friendships and employee associations. A lifelong friend just stops being a lifelong friend, and leaves someone hanging on a limb. Employees commit to a growing corporation and help build the company, then leave, taking clients, co-workers, and legally owned ideas as if they were their own. On the other hand, employees who have helped build the company are cast aside coldly and shown little or no appreciation for their achievements.

The question really being asked by the people left on the

short end of these relationships is, "If someone is no longer meeting my needs, am I justified in no longer meeting theirs?"

Well, the alternative to continually meeting needs is to stop meeting needs. But we have seen where that leads. From cooperation, to retaliation, to domination, to isolation, and finally to termination.

Christ, our Example, made an irreversible commitment to us. He went to the successive points of suffering ridicule, torture, banishment, and finally death for us.

When He was wronged, He didn't retaliate. When He suffered domination, He didn't threaten. When He was isolated, He didn't retreat. Even when His life was terminated, He remained committed (see 1 Peter 2:21-24).

If we want a biblical example of how to handle relationships when people refuse to continue their commitments to meet our needs, Christ is that example.

As Peter continues writing, he carries Christ's example into the human realm so we can understand it. It is as if we are thinking, "Yeah, Christ can commit like that to us, but He's God." So Scripture follows up His example with admonitions about what we should do.

Peter cites husbands and wives. He points out that even though we may be wronged, our commitment should not waver. We should continually meet the other person's needs, so that the least we may do by our actions is give the other person a chance to repent (see 1 Peter 3:1).

Finally, Peter writes, "All of you live in harmony with one another; be sympathetic, love as brothers, be compassionate and humble. Do not repay evil with evil or insult with insult, but with blessing, because to this you were called so that you may inherit a blessing" (1 Peter 3:8-9).

We are told that our commitment is to God, and should be unconditional. This is the kind of commitment He makes to us, to show us how we should act.

Lorraine and I often hear that this sounds so self-righteous. To act in a loving way when we are confronted with pain is to play the "suffering martyr." Peter has a response to this too. "Who is going to harm you if you are eager to do good? But even if you should suffer for what is right, you are blessed. 'Do not fear what they fear; do not be frightened'" (vv. 13-14).

Still, those harmed in relationships have questions. They feel certain that God does not expect them to suffer the pains of their deteriorating relationships. They believe there must be a way out. Yet, Peter goes on to say, "It is better, if it is God's will, to suffer for doing good than for doing evil" (v. 17).

The principle is that there should be a mutual commitment to meeting all needs in the relationship. Just because one person is no longer continuing his commitment, you cannot drop your commitments to him.

No Conditions
This leads us to the third focus of commitment. *The commitment must not be conditional.*

Recently, we invited our next-door neighbors over for popcorn. They have three small children, all preschool age. Our daughter went to her room and brought out several of her stuffed animals for the kids to play with.

One stuffed animal was bigger than the others. All three of the children wanted it. The oldest child was the largest, and she took the big stuffed animal off to a corner and played with it for awhile. When she tired of it, she went over to her little brother and sister and asked them to go downstairs with her to play in our family room.

They didn't want to go. They were happy fooling around with the other stuffed animals. She realized she was going to have to persuade them to come with her. She held out the big stuffed animal to them and said, "If you come down to play with me, I'll let you play with this animal." She was saying that if they would meet her need, she would meet theirs.

Unfortunately, children grow up to be adults operating in the same fashion. We carry the same mentality around about conditional meeting of needs.

As long as we have something that everyone else needs, we will be able to get what we need. We find it difficult to simply give people what they need, without expecting something in return.

Jesus gave us a great example of the unconditional commitment that should be displayed in relationship in His Parable of the Prodigal Son (see Luke 15:11-32). The parable describes a father with two sons. The younger son decided that he was tired of living under the authority of the home. In a purely selfish act, he asked for the portion of the inheritance due him, took it, and left home to go on a wild spending spree.

It is obvious that his only thoughts were for himself. He wasn't thinking about the needs of the family, how his departure might leave them short-handed during harvesttime, or any such thing. He was thinking only of his own immediate needs and desires.

His father could have sat him down and given him a lengthy lecture about maturing and assuming the responsibility of manhood. He could have withheld the money, making a fatherly stipulation that the boy couldn't have his inheritance until he was married. Instead, he met his son's request, and the son left.

After the boy blew all the money and lost all his friends, he began to realize it wasn't so bad at home after all. He decided to return to his father. He planned a proper speech asking for forgiveness and a job as a servant.

"But while he was still a long way off, his father saw him and was filled with compassion for him; he ran to his son, threw his arms around him and kissed him" (v. 20).

The father was still committed to his son. He had never given up the cooperative meeting of his son's needs. He saw right away what his boy needed now and moved to provide it.

Even though the father would have been justified in reprimanding his son for squandering his portion of the inheritance, he met his son's needs instead. The commitment was unconditional. He was willing to love and meet the needs of the son regardless of what the boy did or how he acted.

The boy was reinstated to his position in the family, and the father ordered a great celebration to show his commitment to his son.

Like the father of the prodigal son, we should maintain our commitments unconditionally, whether to children, fellow employees, spouses, or friends. When we make commitments, they should remain firmly on the premise of meeting our partner's needs.

The Five Types of Commitments

One problem with our commitments is that when we say, "I'm really committed to you," it's unclear what we mean. We are just mouthing words unless we know what we are really committed to in the relationship.

Are we committed to share goals? Are we committed to forgive the other person even when he hurts us? Are we committed to continue afterward as if nothing happened? Do we have conditions?

It is impossible to make a commitment without something tangible to define it. Therefore, when you think of commitment to a relationship, you must identify what you are committed to, and what types of commitments you are willing to make.

When a couple marries, they say before witnesses they are committed to each other "as long as we both shall live."

What are they committed to for that long?

In all probability the vow is frequently taken with little clear thinking about the actual meaning behind the commitment. In the final analysis, it is going to be to maintain a cooperative relationship that will enable a relationship to last. The level of commitment determines the longevity of the commitment. Commitments aren't perpetual in themselves.

When I first got into consulting, a businessman told me, "Myron, make sure you always get a signed contract that details everything that's going to be done before you start a consulting project."

For a few years, I faithfully followed that advice. I put into writing the conditions of my contracts.

One day, I was negotiating a contract with a hospital administrator. We got all through and I went back to type up our agreement. I brought it back for him to sign, and he just shook his head.

"Myron, I'd rather shake your hand and have a gentleman's agreement on this. A contract like this is no better than our verbal commitment to each other. We could never get all the conditions down in writing. I want to hear you say we'll hang in there together until we get my needs taken care of."

He told me it's not just what we put in print that determines what we do. We can say what we'll do, and even put it in writing like the rest of the business world. But it is our personal commitment to each other that determines what gets done.

I've made lists for myself, outlining things I'm going to do for Lorraine. Writing those things down isn't what guarantees they'll get done, though the list will help me remember. My commitment to Lorraine is what matters most. Commitment is the motivator of action. Without commitment the list can grow yellow with age.

Our commitments must be positive, outward, and directed to the individual. There are five of these positive commitments we must make in maintaining a cooperative relationship.

Commitment demands that you:
1. Develop and maintain common goals
2. Forgive the mistakes of others in the relationship
3. Forget the times you were wronged
4. Improve the relationship on a continuing basis
5. Put God first and seek to honor Him

Commit to a Common Goal

In 1970, Lorraine and I had been married ten years. As detailed earlier, we were slowly drifting apart because of a lack of common goals. I was deeply involved in pursuing my career and climbing what I thought was the ladder of success.

Every day I found myself spending more time planning and thinking about my career and less and less time planning and thinking about my marriage.

This didn't happen overnight. It was a slowly evolving process. I had interests, dreams, and goals that in the course of my busy work schedule I never stopped to share with Lorraine.

Lorraine also had goals. But since my job was consuming so much of my time, it seemed we never had, or set aside, the time to discuss what we really wanted out of our marriage and our lives.

Consequently, life just happened to us. I always wanted to move to Alaska, because I enjoyed the outdoors. I mentally devised ways to get there. When I was finally offered the opportunity to go to Alaska and implement the organization I dreamed of, I thought it was too good to be true. I saw it as the opportunity to fulfill all my dreams and goals at once.

I was ecstatic the day I announced to Lorraine the offer to make the move.

Since we had not been developing mutual goals, Lorraine had no commitment to my dream and goal. Lorraine was shocked and horrified at the thought.

Her goals, which I knew nothing about, were developing in an entirely different direction. She was committed to maintaining close family ties with her parents. They needed her, and she needed them.

She saw Alaska as completely destructive to her goals. Had Lorraine and I been taking the time to develop common goals, to put God first and seek His will, we could have avoided all the heartache ahead of us.

In our relationships, the first thing to which we should commit is taking the time and doing the work necessary to reach common goals. Failure to make that commitment will ultimately make it impossible to carry out any other personal commitment that we might make in our relationship.

Commit to Forgive

Lorraine and I had not made a commitment to common goals, and therefore she was very hurt when she discovered that my goals were in conflict with hers.

When I announced my goals, she interpreted that as unconcern on my part for her family. Immediately, in the hours that followed, there were many accusations. I accused her of having no interest in my career and our family's future. She accused me of having no concern for her needs and plans.

Consequently, both of us made cutting remarks that hurt deeply. I became angry, and was unwilling to forgive Lorraine for accusing me. For the next few weeks, I dwelled on her statements and became so angry that I didn't see Lorraine as a person anymore.

Failure to forgive becomes a cancer in relationships. It eats away at our commitments to the other person.

I started using Lorraine's cutting remarks to justify my own stubborn position. I told myself that if Lorraine didn't care for my needs, I wouldn't care for hers.

My being unwilling to forgive made it easy to demand my own way, which I did.

Scripture tells us, "Do not let the sun go down while you are still angry" (Eph. 4:26). In writing this, the Apostle Paul showed he realized the necessity of our being committed to forgive each other if we are going to maintain cooperative relationships.

Commit to Forget

It is one thing to tell people, "I forgive you." It is another to say, "I will forget what you did."

We must be committed not only to forgive but to forget that we were wronged. To forget is to put out of our memory that something even happened.

Hezekiah, King of Judah, once wrote of God, "You have put all my sins behind Your back" (Isa. 38:17).

Unless we are willing to do the same with the sins of those who wrong us—to forget as well as forgive—we tend to keep score. The relationship will then deteriorate into a game of one-upmanship.

So long as Lorraine and I were unwilling to forget the wrongs, we were unable to focus on each other's needs. If she wronged me, I kept reminding myself of it. I didn't forgive her, and I didn't forget either.

I kept carrying along the past, including all the hurt. Instead of being motivated to meet Lorraine's needs, I was motivated to return hurt to Lorraine. I wanted to retaliate.

Retaliation relationships begin because we are unwilling to forget the wrongs done to us. We conclude we have a right to get back at the other and "equal" the score.

If you have any question about whether you have forgiven and forgotten the wrongs committed against you, evaluate your present conflicts. Do you constantly bring up past mistakes that you haven't forgotten? Failure to put them behind your back is just like reopening an old wound. If your relationship is to be a cooperative one, it is imperative you not reopen old wounds. There will be plenty of new hurts in the relationship; don't keep the old hurts too.

Commit To Improve

Lorraine and I have observed in our relationship that it is very easy to become complacent and to think we already have a good marriage. It is easy to believe we know how the other feels and to neglect sitting down to discuss things.

The hardest work we do in our lives is the work involved in continually building and strengthening our relationships. It is an unending task, like pulling weeds out of the garden. When I was a kid growing up on the farm, every Saturday morning before I did anything else, my job was to go out to the garden to pull all the weeds. Then I could play.

We need to do this in our relationships too. Unless we work at our relationships continually, the weeds grow bigger and harder to pull. Eventually, it will take a major part of our day to get rid of just one patch of weeds, because we have to dig down so deep to get the roots out.

Relationships require unending attention. We must forgive, forget, and then make sure there aren't any other problems in the relationship that can cause us pain.

Problems in relationships will always arise. It is a lifelong reality of human contact—even if we live in a cooperative style. We will never reach the stage in our relationships when they no longer require maintenance.

We must continually focus on improving our communication, continually focus on meeting each other's needs, continually focus on developing new mutual goals, and continually focus on forgiving and forgetting.

In an earlier chapter, we discovered that relationships are constantly changing. They either improve or degenerate. When we stop working to improve them, degeneration and deterioration take over. Don't let it happen. Commit yourself to improving your relationships.

Commit to God

By far the most important commitment we make as individuals is to God. When we commit to Him, we also commit to His laws of effective relationships, such as we've discussed throughout this book. He is also committed to us in a way that teaches us how we should be committed to others.

Earlier, we observed that six of the Ten Commandments focus on maintaining human relationships. The other four enable us to maintain our relationships to God.

All of the commandments are relationship oriented. That is basically what being a human being is all about! And we have plenty of help. God's Word is filled with challenges, commands, and examples of good relationship styles to follow and bad ones to avoid.

To violate the Bible's relationship principles guarantees problems in our relationships. To maintain healthy, cooperative relationships, we should find out what God urges us, shows us, and commands us to do.

I challenge you to make a commitment to God and his biblical principles of relationships. Dig them out for yourself.

I've discovered in my own experience that God's Word is the best source of help available anywhere for solving relationship problems. After all, He's the designer of the relationship system that makes all of us dependent on each other. It only makes sense that He's the primary source for maintaining relationships too.

The thesis of this book—and God's basic principle for our maintaining effective relationships—is: "Each of us should please his neighbor for his good, to build him up" (Rom. 15:2).

As we make that our commitment, we will find all of our relationships taking on new life and new meaning.

A Final Thought

It is never to late to start applying the principles outlined in this book, and to begin rebuilding your shattered and weakened relationships into strong, cooperative ones.

Don't miss out on the exciting life God has for you by allowing yourself to be deceived into thinking it is too late to try.

An elderly man said to me at the conclusion of a relationship seminar, "If I'd known these things forty years ago, my life would have been a much happier one. But it's too late to try now."

It's never too late. The choice is up to you. And the options are clear. You can either follow the world's philosophy of "me first" and through your own selfishness destroy the good life God has planned for you, or you can follow God's laws of relationships and commit to meeting the needs of others.

If you take the second route, you will discover the truth of Jesus' commandment, "Give, and it will be given to you. A good measure, pressed down, shaken together, and running over, will be poured into your lap. For with the measure you use, it will be measured to you" (Luke 6:38).

I have proved in my own life the truth of that principle as it applies to relationships. You can too.

Conclusion

Let's consider here a few of the questions most often asked at our seminars.

What could or should a person in isolation do to restore the relationship?

The very first step is to evaluate your commitment to the relationship. If it is a work relationship and your commitment is only "until I find something else when jobs are easier to find," then the energy required to move the relationship from isolation back to cooperation is much greater than your commitment. Therefore it is probably not worth your effort. You might as well leave.

On the other hand, if your commitment is in marriage "until death do us part," you and your spouse have real hope. It is worth every ounce of strength you have to make the relationship not only last but be enjoyable for both of you, as well as for those whose lives you touch. Above all, you must begin to communicate, though that is the hardest thing for a person in the isolation style to do. But this is a must. You simply have to force yourself to communicate.

Scripture guides us in how we are to communicate. Speak the truth; be honest. Don't be angry, but rather have a spirit of love. Give, rather than always expecting to receive. Build up the other person in place of tearing down. (See Eph. 4:25-31.) "Be kind and compassionate to one another, forgiving each other, just as in Christ God forgave you" (v. 32).

The steps for a person moving out of isolation are: be committed to the relationship; force yourself to communicate, and be consistent.

Lorraine, how long did it take before you really trusted Myron again?

Years. Restoring a relationship is like hiking in the mountains: you can go down hill rapidly with little effort, but the climb back up takes lots of energy and is a very slow process.

What can I do to make a person in a particular relationship style change?

Nothing. It is not your responsibility to make another person change. Your responsibility is to do your part to change. It is God's responsibility to change the other person or lead him to respond to your change.

Scripture tells us that a person can be won without a word from us as they observe our respectful behavior. (See 1 Peter 3:1-2.) This particular passage is written to wives, because we especially need it, but it is also a principle of relationships.

Once you do something to make someone else respond in a particular manner, that becomes manipulation.

If another person in relationship with you needs to change, I can suggest only two steps for you to take:

Step 1—Pray a lot, expecting God to work.

Step 2—Accept responsibility for your own behavior and changes you need to make, leaving the responsibility to deal with the other party up to God.